POOL CUES, BEER BOTTLES, & BASEBALL BATS

POOL CUES, CUES, BEER

Animal's Guide to Improvised Weapons for Self-Defense and Survival

BOTTLES, & BASEBALL BATS

Marc "Animal" MacYoung

PALADIN PRESS
BOULDER, COLORADO

Also by Marc "Animal" MacYoung:

Cheap Shots, Ambushes, and Other Lessons:
A Down and Dirty Book on Streetfighting and Survival

Fists, Wits, and a Wicked Right:
Surviving on the Wild Side of the Street

Knives, Knife Fighting, and Related Hassles:
How to Survive a *Real* Knife Fight

Pool Cues, Beer Bottles, & Baseball Bats:
Animal's Guide to Improvised Weapons
for Self-Defense and Survival

Violence, Blunders, and Fractured Jaws:
Advanced Awareness Techniques and Street Etiquette

Floor Fighting: Stompings, Maimings, and Other Things
to Avoid When a Fight Goes to the Floor

Pool Cues, Beer Bottles, and Baseball Bats:
Animal's Guide to Improvised Weapons for Self-Defense and Survival
by Marc "Animal" MacYoung

Copyright © 1990 by Marc MacYoung

ISBN 0-87364-545-6
Printed in the United States of America

Published by Paladin Press, a division of
Paladin Enterprises, Inc., P.O. Box 1307,
Boulder, Colorado 80306, USA.
(303) 443-7250

Direct inquiries and/or orders to the above address.

Illustrations by Marc MacYoung

This one's dedicated to all my old runnin' buddies, friends, partners, bros, and amigos, for all the times we had, are having, and will have.

Contents

Preface

Good knowledge comes from bad experiences.
—American provincial wisdom

You know, I don't write these books so people can go out and kick somebody's ass. In fact, I write them so people don't go out and get their asses *kicked.*

This may sound like an odd way of promoting this book, but actually it's not. You could use the information in this book to go out and harm people because you're pissed off, or you could use it to keep your ass out of the morgue. I personally hope it's the latter.

I am not some hotshot martial artist here to show you all the fancy moves he knows; nor am I some type of mercenary commando who's going to show you three thousand ways to kill. (I admit that I have training in both fields, but that's neither here nor there.) I am not a cop either, although I have worked as both event security and, at times, bouncer.

What I am is an old outlaw. A streetfighter, if you will. This isn't something you really train for, it's something you live, sometimes not by choice. The outlaw trail is like the path of the wolf: it teaches you much about life and people and gives you an understanding of how things work. It can also be an insane, lonely, and vicious path.

This book is designed to give you an idea of what you might encounter in the area of fighting. I am not (as my publisher puts it) "some theory-spouting pogue" when it comes to this department. In my life, I have walked on both sides of the law and sanity. I have been mellow and I have been rowdy. I have lived in mansions and in my car. I've been a foreman, drug dealer, manager, muscle, truck driver, construction worker, artist, mover, shit shoveler, writer (same thing), and a whole host of other things. I have ridden through both heaven and hell, and I have the memories and scars to prove it. I have seen both life and death (sometimes too much of both), and I know what both look like. In other words, I've seen a slice-and-a-half of life.

All of my experiences add up to a real different way of looking at life than most folks'. This is what happens when you decide to live outside of what you were taught was "normal." Most people try to draw lines to where things begin and end. They try to make nice, neat little boxes that put everything in its place. It would be nice if that were the way things actually worked, but it's not. Things are more interrelated and connected than we were taught by society when we were growing up. We have been trained to pretend that all of life is a static, dead, sectional machine, in the actual operation of which we have no part. We are told that if we perform certain mechanical actions, certain results will follow. Our society would like us to believe that all you have to do is turn a key and the rest is taken care of by some other system; you have no control of or responsibility to the whole process. This may be true in specific situations, but in the big picture of life it's not. There is no such thing as "you just do this and this happens."

This is especially true in the area of self-defense. You can't just learn the moves and expect to survive a real streetfight. You have to be able to look forward, backward, sideways, this-a-way and that-a-way to be adept at self-defense. Fighting is more complicated than people would like it to be, and at the same time, it's simpler.

I'm going to talk about things in this book that may appear to have nothing to do with weapons, or, for that matter, self-defense. What these things do have something to do with is survival—yours. Self-defense is awareness, not the ability to beat somebody up. Knowing how to beat somebody up is knowing how to fight. If the world didn't have things called cheap shots, ambushes, blind shots, traps, muggings, egos, and revenge, that would be enough. Since the world *does* have these things, just being able to fight isn't enough. Fighting can't really protect you from these things; awareness can.

What most people are taught as self-defense is, in my mind, the equivalent of teaching somebody to drive without teaching them about the brakes. While it is possible to drive with no brakes (I've done it), it's better to know about them. It's better still to use them.

This is why I write survival books rather than self-defense books. Self-defense books only show you what to *do* in *certain* situations. Survival books show you how to *think* in *various* situations.

Most self-defense books only tell you one approach to dealing with a situation—that is, how to hit the guy once he's jumped out of the bushes and attacked you. Nine times out of ten, they also teach techniques that rely on the guy being off balance and sloppy and standing there like a wooden dummy while you supposedly rip his arm off (good luck). They don't tell you what to do if something goes wrong with a move (which happens a lot); nor do they mention what goes on before or after a fight. All those things are bad enough, but in my opinion, what's worse is they don't give you any idea of how to avoid the situation in the first place.

Contrary to what you may think, most shit doesn't happen in jump-out-of-the-bushes-type situations. More often than not, you'll be at a bar, party, whatever, and somebody will start giving you the hard eye. The next thing you know, fists are flying. You may be Joe Karate, but a beer bottle can settle anybody's hash real fuckin' quick.

What you should know better than flashing feet and terrifying *kiais* is the fact that you spoke to the guy before the shit went down. Knowing what is going on at this point is more important than being able to break bricks while making funny sounds. There's a reason I say this. Bricks don't hit back. Nor do they pull knives out of nowhere and stab the black belt who's going to break them in half. People do. This is why knowing what's going on is as important, if not more so, than knowing how to kick ass.

These are the things I'm going to teach you in this book. Maybe you won't have to bleed to learn them like I did, 'cause let's face it, *fighting hurts.* Truth is, it's unpredictable and not much fun (especially if you lose). Most people don't have the experience it takes to know what to watch out for; and you can get seriously hurt in this business for not knowing something like that. Every now and then, though, you gotta fight.

That's why I wrote this book—for those people who can keep their eyes open and aren't afraid to look at the world in a different way than they're used to. If you're looking to get by and not get hurt by some sneaky son of a bitch, then this book is for you. If you're just looking for ways to kick the shit out of people, this book will probably bore and confuse the shit out of you.

Like in all my books, I have to stress something up front. I don't know everything there is to know about fighting. Nobody does. What I'm telling you here are things that I have used to save my life more than once. There are things I don't know about life, the universe, and all related crap. But what I do know comes from personal experience and research. There are also things I know but ain't telling. (I don't want to get locked up.)

I'll probably say things here that you might not agree with. Fine. No law says you have to agree with everything I say. I don't talk with thunder-and-shit-marble; you don't have to do everything I say. You're the one trying to live your life. I'm busy livin' mine. All I'm doing here is offering advice, not preaching gospel.

What I'm trying to say is, I'm no glorified expert. You can't get a Ph.D. in life anyway. You can deserve it, but nobody is giving away the diplomas. My ego isn't going to get bruised if you think I'm off base with what I'm saying. It's okay. You're a thinking person, and it's your right to think your own thoughts and do what you feel is right. What I do may not work for you, and I know that. It's from that standpoint that I give you the advice in this book. Get what you can out of it and forget the rest.

By the way, this isn't a book on precise techniques. It consists of a weird blend of 1) the basics you'll need to know in order to teach yourself about improvised weapons, and 2) the advanced details that are usually left out of formal training, but that you'll need to know about if you use this stuff in a real fight. This book is written for the person who has never picked up a weapon before in his life but wants to learn; for the person who is learning and wants to advance; and for the old streetfighter who hadn't thought about it this way before. Any way you cut it, this book is written for people who want to stay alive in dangerous situations. So if you want to learn about improvised weapons, this is the *theory* behind them that'll actually make learning to use them easier. If you know weapon techniques already, this will broaden your knowledge so you can apply it to other types of weapons, and it'll fine-tune the stuff you know. If you're an old-timer, you'll laugh, 'cause we all know what kind of situations this information comes from.

Oh, by the way, if you've read my other books, you already know I screw around a lot. If you haven't, be warned. I'd fuck around at my own funeral (that is, unless I miss it altogether, which I have every intention of trying to do).

Serious Shit

Red Dawg paused over his beer and fixed his supposed-to-be-blue (more often than not bloodshot) eyes on me in macho disbelief. "Man, I'd admit that I jerk off before I copped to getting beat up with a hairbrush," he said.

I laughed, pulled the woman next to me closer, and took a hit of beer. "Fuck man, I cop to both, I ain't proud." We all chuckled and proceeded with our goal of seeing just how far off the ground we could raise hell. (We managed to get it somewhere around two feet—not a world's record or anything, but not bad for an improvised riot.)

Years later, I look back at that conversation and realize a few things. The Dawg's attitude was pretty much what most people feel about improvised weapons, which is something along the lines of, "It couldn't happen to me!" I hate to break up the barbecue folks, but yes it could. *In fact, generally speaking, most injuries that people suffer from physical confrontations are because of the "unexpected."* What's more, most people who come out intact know how to deal with—and deal out—the unex-

1

pected. If you're into breathing, you will not only take this little tidbit to heart, you will apply it to your way of life.

Starting with the big picture and working our way over to improvised weapons, let's look at what I mean by "deal with" and "deal out" the unexpected. The Special Forces are revered as one of our top fighting units. Yet, they, the Rangers, SEALs, and LRRPs rely not so much on raw firepower but correct information, stealth, options, planning, and SURPRISE!

It has been my personal experience that ninjutsu isn't really that hot of a fighting form. But it doesn't matter, 'cause unless you're aware, you never see the motherfucker until it's way too late. Muggings often happen the same way. Most people realize something is wrong too late to do them any good! In a barroom brawl, if the guy is an old hand, who knows where the fuck it's going to come from?

People ask me what fighting style I use. I tell them PIBU. It stands for a pitcher of beer (well, actually, a specific kind of beer, but if I put it in print they'll sue my ass off). The motto of any PIBU master is, "Either we're going to sit down and drink it together or I'm going to bean the motherfucker with it." Martial artists think I'm joking about this. Old streetfighters get the "Oh, you know about that trick" grin when they hear it. (I liked the guy who said, "I prefer MUBU. That's mug of beer. Since they started making plastic pitchers, PIBU hurts less.")

This is why I always stress that there is a difference between the mat and the alley. In a dojo, nobody is going to ambush you, bust a chair across your teeth, or knock a trash can into your footwork. You can also pretty much count out the chance of getting chain-whipped. However, I speak from experience when I say these things do happen in alleys and bars.

If you think anything other than a toe-to-toe slug-out is chicken shit and wouldn't work on you, I suggest you go join a martial arts class and stay in tournament competition and out of real fights, because in the real world, people with that attitude end up in jail, hospitalized, or dead.

If, however, from left field, you have recently gotten a chain wrapped around your face and you are now open to learning a new thing or two, sit down, get comfy, crack a beer, and let's talk.

When people think about weapons, they generally think of guns, knives, and occasionally, clubs. They also are prone to think of a sense of finality: "It's over, I won." I mean, we've all seen the movies. Bad guy gets shot dead, good guy rescues the heroine, and they go off so she can give him a blow job. Yippee! Everybody is happy. Bad news folks. Unless you use a weapon right, the shit is just beginning! Let's look at some basics here.

1) *Weapons can be used without it being final!* People often think only "lethal" when they think of weapons. Any tool that is used to aid and abet knocking the shit out of someone is considered a weapon! Capisce? You have to widen your definition of what constitutes a weapon. In my time, I have been clobbered by or attacked with hairbrushes, a pot, rope, scissors, beer bottles, pens, a cat, tables and chairs, pool cues, shuriken, playing cards, keys, razor blades, rocks, a candleholder, shoes, a cup of Coke, and, of course, chains. I have used leaves, dirt, the water from a dog dish, a shirt, a belt, trash cans, paint scrapers, beer, orange juice, spit, and many of the things I previously listed, to

open conversations. Many of these serve to knock you off balance or mildly hurt you so you'll choke and your attacker can get in there with something more serious. Others are more serious by themselves. You don't know the meaning of the word pain until you've had a busted nose or a kneecap blown out on you. Then again, a busted jaw ain't no fuckin' picnic either.

2) *Weapons can be final.* Human beings are one of the weirdest blends of fragile and tougher'n shit that you'll ever see. There is no predicting what will happen with them. I have seen people knocked out with one punch, and I've also seen people get pool cues busted over their heads with no apparent effect. I've seen people get shot and just keep going; I also know about the knock-'em-down effects of some guns. I've seen people stabbed multiple times and keep going, and I've seen corpses with just one little hole in them. I've seen people take a ball shot and shrivel up like a worm on a frying pan. I've also gotten kicked in the balls and gone into a cold fury. The worst damage I've ever done to people often felt like I had just barely touched them, yet they went to the hospital. I've also given people my absolute best shot and had them just look at me. (Fortunately, I have always been a fast runner.) All of this should point to the fact that there is no way to predict what will happen during violence. You might hit someone in just the right way (or wrong, depending on your point of view) and kill them. Or everything you have may not work to stop the motherfucker. That is why I stress the next basic.

3) *There ain't no such thing as a guarantee in a fight.* It's the macho fucks who keep thinking that because they're so rough and tough they can't be hurt. Unless they modify this attitude and start

looking into the shadows, they have a life expectancy of about five years. In case you hadn't noticed, dead is a long-term thing. Crippled ain't no two-week stint either. The absolute best you can hope for is to keep your eyes and mind open when it comes to fighting. In any fight, you'll sustain damage any way you cut it, but you can minimize it if you're alert. A major portion of why I'm still alive is because I always imagined my opponent was better than I was and had about six tricks up his sleeve that he was going to try and pull on me. It has kept me from getting fat and lazy. It also has kept me breathing. Some guy once said, "There are more people who are still living because they overestimated their opponent than there are people who underestimated their opponent."

4) *Weapons can get long-term ugly.* Losing the fight, cops, hospitals, prison, and revenge seekers all make the aftermath of weapon fighting a real pain in the ass. If you nail somebody with a bottle and he ends up in the hospital, that is assault with a deadly weapon (keeping in mind basic rule #2, the guy might die). In case you hadn't noticed, there are a lot of guys in jail for a thing called murder. Jails are for the guys who lived. There are also a lot of people in graveyards for something called death. You may not always be the one swinging the bottle. If you've got a hot head, you'd better learn to control it before you get into this territory. With weapons, there is no room for "loose cannons on deck." The people who live and stay free are the ones who think before they act.

You may want to rip the shit out of someone, but stop and think about it for a minute. Is it worth the rest of your life? We are talking about weapons here, folks, and that's what they can spell.

Now, if the guy has blown his cool already and is coming at you with a weapon, that argument becomes sort of academic. Or if the guy's trying to mug, rape, rob, or generally annoy you, it's a free-for-all, and you had damn well better know how to wing it with whatever is around you.

The truth is that you really have to keep your shit wired tight when you're talking about weapons. Knowing this stuff can save your life; using it the wrong way can end it.

The Basics

I've always been allergic to both road rash and getting my teeth kicked in. This is why I've tried to avoid both with awareness and reflexes.

On a motorcycle, you can usually spot potential trouble by watching the front wheels of cars around you. The wheels of a car will begin to turn something like a second before the car follows. To hell with signals and position—the wheels will tell you what is about to happen. There are a lot of squids around who don't know that little bit of information. (A Los Angeles phenomenon. Young, sleek, yuppie jocks, wearing no protection on Japanese muscle machines. These kids are hyped up on looks, high horsepower, high hormones, and a belief in their own immortality.) They'll learn . . . or they'll die. The thing is, that simple bit of information comes from one of two places—either personal experience or an old-timer who tells you about it.

Most people think basics are things like how to stay on a motorcycle or how to hold a knife. The basics I'm talking about are things like watching the wheels or knowing how someone carries a concealed

7

knife. These are the things that are often overlooked
by martial art instructors.

Basics come in two different forms: keys and
patterns. Keys are specific things to watch for.
Patterns consist of a string of related keys. What
they actually come down to is a way of thinking
about things and events that will tip you off as to
what is coming down the pikeway or will be in a bit.
Let's look at it this way. You're walking down a path
and you hear a vibrating buzz. Guess what? You've
just found a rattlesnake! Surprise! This is what I
mean by "knowing what to look for." (Okay, so you
hear a rattlesnake. Its an analogy, alright! Don't get
technical.) The rattle is the key to knowing there is a
poisonous snake around.

Patterns take a little longer to explain. Let's say
you have a friend at work. His name is . . . um . . .
Billy Joe. You and Billy Joe usually go out after
work and have a couple. Fine so far. Okay, Billy Joe
has a girlfriend. Her name is Linda. She and Billy
Joe don't exactly get into fights, but every now and
then Linda tears into ol' Billy Joe. The next day,
Billy Joe is just not quite right. It's nothing that you
can really put your finger on, but he's not acting
right—short answers, tenseness around the mouth,
narrow eyes, and just a general air of him being
about as cuddly as a porcupine. If you ask, you
might find out what happened the night before. If
you don't ask, it just looks like he got up on the
wrong side of the bed.

Well, what the hell, we all have off days, right?
So off you go with Billy Joe to have your customary
after-work drink. There you are in the bar, and
somebody looks cross-eyed at Billy Joe. The next
thing you know, Billy Joe is in a fight with the guy.
Shit, bad news. Okay, the situation is resolved.

Until the next time. Next time, it's a different guy, but this time, he has friends. Three guesses as to who's about to get involved in Billy Joe's little problem. I'll give you a hint. He looks amazingly like you and is reading a book at this very moment.

This is what I mean by "patterns." They're preprogrammed ways of thinking that result in predictable behavior in certain situations. Here, the pattern is as follows. Linda has a rough day at work. That night, in an obvious case of "kick the dog," Linda tears into Billy Joe over something trivial. The next day, Billy Joe is grouchy at work. Then, when you two go out after work, he gets into a fight.

If this happens only once, it's no big thing. But if it happens a second time, it might be. If it happens a third time, you've now got a full-fledged pattern. There's a motto I learned somewhere in my travels that I'd like to share with you. It's a good rule of thumb to define patterns. "*Once is interesting. Twice is happenstance. Three times, it's a game!*" Patterns are things that happen that you really couldn't prove in court, but damn it, you know they happen!

Usually, if you confront a person with this sort of thing, they'll either deny it flat out, or they'll profess ignorance to anything like that. The latter response is actually true more often than not. Most people not only have blind spots they can't see, but they aren't aware that they can't see them. Way too much human action originates from these blind spots. Since most people don't even know they got 'em, you can bet that they're real blind to actions coming out from 'em.

For example, Billy Joe really loves Linda, and he's not the sort who likes to fight with his old lady. So instead of taking his anger out on her, he goes out and gets in a fight. This is his blind spot. He doesn't see the connection between what Linda did last night and tonight's fight. This connection does exist, though, and you need to know about it or you'll get dragged in, too. In a sense, these people really don't know what's going on. They're just following their program without thinking about what they're doing. Sometimes their shit is aimed at you; other times you just get splattered by it.

Others, however, know they're up to something and are like kids with their hands not quite in—but real close to—the cookie jar. These people are definitely aiming at you. Nothing has ever been overt, but lots of stuff has happened. In one way of phrasing it, you could say that "nothing is exactly wrong, but something sure'n hell ain't right." If you confront them, they'll act as if it's a total surprise. It's like the response of the ax murderer who got stopped in a rented car. When the cops asked him about the ax and revolvers in the trunk, he said (and I quote), "Damned if I know, but you can be sure I'll never rent another car from Avis." Yeah right, guy. Little things happen with these people. Alone, they don't mean much, but if you string 'em together, they don't paint a pretty picture. As a matter of fact it looks exactly like a major setup.

For the most part, in these setups, your being "reasonable" is necessary in order for them to work. (There are other types of setups, though, which rely on you blowing your cool; so if you have a hot temper, you have to watch out for these. They can be used against you real well.) You have to understand that there are times you can't "be reasonable" if you want to survive. Because most people don't want to look like an asshole, they let this sort of shit slide. I have no trouble admitting that I can be a flaming asshole. If I spot this kind of shit, I stand up and raise hell about it. Calling the ball is the best way to stop this kind of shit from going down. If people say that I'm being unreasonable, my response is, "Yeah, I may be wrong, but then again I may be right" (or, "Don't piss down my back and tell me it's raining.")

I don't start swinging when I spot this sort of shit (usually 'cause I spot it early these days), but I draw a serious line and tell them that, reasonable or not, if they cross it, I will start swinging. Usually this line is the next step of the pattern I just spotted. If it was a mistake and I misread it as a pattern, there's no blood spilled. This is what keeps me popular. If I read it right, it lets the guy know he's been spotted and targeted. Believe me, that little red dot of light is a great deterrent to people who do this shit on purpose. They know that a slug is going to end up where that little laser is pointed, and it's pointed right at their chest.

Now, I don't want you to take what I've said as *carte blanche* to go out and be a prick and react like everything is a setup. (Since we live in a self-adjusting universe, anyone who did would find out why that's not such a hot idea. It's a given law—there's always someone faster on the draw. Learn that and you might live long enough to lie to your grandkids.) You do need to know, however, that occasionally someone is going to try and set you up. Fifty percent of what goes on is unrelated to you personally. Of the remaining half about 20 percent is unintentional, or the result of pure mechanical process. Another 20 percent is pure SNAFU. This means that about 90 percent of all the things that go on around you fall under Einstein's Theory of Reality: R=Shit Happens. There still remains that 10 percent, however.

It is that 10 percent you have to be aware of.

This is where the patterns *really* matter, because they're aimed at you. That other 90 percent can nail you pretty hard, but theoretically, everybody has the same chance of getting clobbered by it. We all get our turn in the barrel now and then. Life's a bitch that way, but that's how it goes. That remaining 10 percent is somebody trying specifically to red dot you.

In time, when you've gotten the hang of looking for your 10 percent, you can begin to see other patterns in the 90 percent. These are things that aren't after you specifically but will nail anybody standing where it's about to come down. It's sort of like accidently having a safe dropped on you from a building. When you are looking out for yourself, you learn that a good rule of thumb is not to walk under safes hanging out of windows. The guy who dropped it didn't have it out for you, but you'd be just as dead as if he had. The nice thing is patterns in the 90 percent are easier to avoid than those aimed at you. All you have to do is know better than to be in the wrong place at the wrong time.

In other words, if you start keeping your eyes open, you can generally not only keep from getting nailed by your shit, but you can keep from getting splattered by other people's.

Now, you may be wondering why I just bored you with that long-winded sermon. Something along the lines of, "What the fuck does this have to do with improvised weapons?" The answer is, EVERYTHING!

Spotting the key points of a violent pattern that is starting to go down is the only real way to keep from getting your head knocked in by somebody! In a more specific sense, it's understanding what the pattern of a general category of weapon looks like that will keep you from getting creamed when someone tries to use an object in that manner. Fortunately, with a little practice these patterns are easily recognizable.

Look at it this way. You're doing a job and you have a bitch of a situation. Unknown to you, there's a tool that makes this job a whole hell of a lot easier. First, you have to know that such a tool exists, then you have to find one, then you get to use it. In the same way, you have to know these basic keys and patterns in the first place. (That's what this chapter is for.) Once you know they exist, you have to go out and find them. (That's what the rest of the book is about.) Then you get to use them in your daily life.

This I why I have just stood on a soapbox and yapped my head off about basics, keys, patterns, and all that shit. You now know the tool exists. Now let's go out and find it.

F.I.I.K.
L.F.O.[1]

*It is a thing o'
beauty, despite
its purpose.*
—A movie-crew
saying

This chapter will acquaint you with the basic types of improvised weapons and the key things they share. Most improvised weapons fall into three main categories. These are:

A	B	C
Range	**Type**	**Construction**
Projectile	Bludgeon	Fixed
Close range	Impact	Flexible
	Edged	
	Trapping	
	Point	
	Ripper	

It works like a Chinese restaurant menu—one from Column A, two from Column B, and one from Column C. You can mix and match to come up with combos, especially with Column B. (Egg rolls and

[1] Pronounced Fickle Foe, which means, "Fuck If I Know, Let's Find Out."

rice come with them all, but soy sauce is extra.)

Let's look at it this way. Here we have a beer bottle. There is some guy in your face. You reach over and grab the bottle by the neck with your thumb against the body. When you whap the guy upside the head with your beer bottle, you are using it:

    A) at close range
    B) as a bludgeon
    C) as a fixed weapon.

If someone is coming at you from across the room with a chair, you should pick up the bottle and throw it. It then becomes:

    A) a projectile
    B) an impact weapon
    C) fixed.

If, however, you just haul off and backhand the guy with the bottle in your hand, you're using it:

    A) at close range
    B) as an impact weapon
    C) as a fixed weapon.

But what if you grab it and smash it against the side of a building first? It then becomes:

    A) close range
    B) an edge or point, possibly both
    C) flexible.

The reason it becomes a flexible rather than fixed weapon is that bottles are unpredictable. Flexible generally means a weapon that changes shape during use, like a chain or a whip. But in this case, it means something that may fall apart in your hand, which a freshly broken bottle just might decide to do. Technically, it falls somewhere between fixed and flexible, which makes it just plain fuckin' unpredictable to both attacker and attackee. Also, the way it breaks determines whether it becomes an edge weapon (slash) or a point weapon (stab). Sometimes it's both (edge/point).

So, you begin to see what sort of variations you have to watch out for. Most things can be used against you in a variety of ways. You must be able to spot the changing circumstances to predict what will happen next. For example, say some guy swings a pool cue at you. You dodge and he misses. The pool cue breaks on the pool table. What has changed? Well, for one, he attacked first with A) a distance weapon, B) a bludgeon, and C) a fixed weapon. If he's hip, he can now attack you with the stub, which, depending on how it broke, has now become either A) close range, B) a point, and C) fixed, or A) a distance weapon, B) a point, and C) a fixed weapon. In other words, he's either going to try and jab your ass with an ice pick or a spear. In this instance, pretend you're Dracula and get the fuck away from the stake. It's time for your beer bottle to go projectile mode.

Now, let's look at a set of keys on a chain. How long is the chain? Let's say two to three feet. (Yes, they do come that long; what do you think those zoot suiters were doing?) That makes it:

    A) a distance weapon
    B) an impact/ripper
    C) flexible.

Now that you have a general idea of how this stuff translates into reality, let's look specifically at how the various types of improvised weapons fit into these categories.

Sometimes they are directly out of a Robin Hood movie, like quarterstaves, shields, maces, spears, and darts. (Yes, darts. They used to be a Celtic weapon, around two feet long and weighing about three pounds. If they hit you, they'd fuck you up pretty good. They've since mellowed out and evolved into a pub pastime.)

Other weapons seem to be something out of "Kung Fu" or a Chop-Socky flick. They include shuriken, yawara sticks, nunchucks, and that sort of stuff.

Others will just plain old sound weird until you think about it for a bit—things like tiger claws, boomerangs, monkey balls, and yo-yos. (Yes, the Filipino weapon. It was used for hunting and war.)

First, let's dissect Column A.

Distance Weapons. Anything you can use when you're anywhere from two to five feet from the guy who has one. These include spears, quarterstaves, chains, baseball bats, canes, yo-yos, nunchucks, chairs, and anything else you can think of to keep the asshole away from you.

Projectiles. Anything that can be thrown, fris-beed, chucked, or lobbed to either impact, stab, or cut your opponent. These include bottles, rocks, darts, shuriken, pool balls, trash can lids, ashtrays, improvised spears, playing cards, and, of course, cats. (You think I'm joking? Tabby lands with four little buzz saws going full speed.)

Close-range Weapons. Anything you would be in danger of from about two-and-a-half feet or closer. These are knives, bottles, billy clubs, blackjacks, tire irons, razor blades, banjo picks, keys, yawara sticks, ashtrays, peanut bowls, shoes, hairbrushes, pots, and pans. Most of these things can alternate between hand-held and projectile real quick, which kind of extends their range, but fortunately, only once.

From Column B, you can either have individual units or you can combine them. Individually, you have:

Bludgeon. This is anything that clubs. Going from big to little, you have quarterstaves, bats, sticks, canes, small articles of furniture, billy clubs, bottles, and of course 2 x 4s in this category. Also included are certain mace variations like nunchucks, blackjacks, chains, and yo-yos.

Impact Weapons. Except when they are thrown, impact weapons basically vary from bludgeons in that they are used primarily for making the hand harder than it normally is. With a club, you're striking with the club; with an impact weapon, you're still striking with your hand, but it's got some artificial aid. Brass knuckles, punch rings, yawara sticks, rolls of coin, and lead-lined punch gloves are all good examples of what I mean. When thrown, impact weapons bump you a good one.

Edged Weapons. Knives aren't the only thing in this category, although they do make up the bulk of it. Specifically speaking, an edged weapon is for slashing rather than stabbing. Here, you have knives, razors, certain types of broken bottles, broken glass, and occasionally, sharpened belt buckles.

Trapping Weapons. These are rare unless you encounter someone who is well-trained. Then you're in some serious shit. A trapping weapon is anything that catches your opponent's blow and either binds it long enough for blows to get by or drags him off balance. When they're used right, canes, ropes, chains, men's ties, belts, bar stools, articles of clothing, and whips all serve as trappers. I once threw a punch at a guy who used a pot to trap me—silly, but true.

Point Weapons. Like their brothers the edged weapons, these are real cocksuckers to deal with. The difference is they aren't for slashing—they're for stabbing, and stab they will. Ice picks, broken bottles, broken pool cues, certain types of stilettos, sharpened hair picks/combs, and darts all fall into this category.

Rippers. (Jack baby, long time no see. Now, back into the time warp, dude.) Rippers put holes in your flesh, but they don't do it cleanly. In fact, they either rip, gouge, tear, or puncture—all of which can fuck up your suntan. They also leave little wet spots on the carpet, which are a bitch to get out. In the ripper department, you have keys, tin can lids, the back edge and tips of knives, banjo picks, saws, jagged glass, and scissors.

Those are the individual categories. It really gets interesting when you begin to combine them.

Bludgeon/ripper. This could be anything from a board with nails sticking out of it to an honest-to-God mace. (I and a few of my friends used to make them. We'd make the component parts in metal shop in school and assemble them at home. I know a cop who pulled a guy over, and when he asked him to step out of his car, one fell onto the street. The guy looked at the cop and said, "I don't know who that belongs to." Audacity. Sometimes it works, and other times it's too ridiculous to believe.) Also in this category, you'll find metal-headed canes, keys on a chain (although it's related more to a flail than a mace), rakes, shovels, and a whole host of other gardening tools.

Impact/rippers. God, the list is endless! Those that you're more likely to encounter are punch rings, keys held in the hand, anything that breaks when someone hits you with it (like a coffee cup), a long list of hand-held tools, thrown broken bottles, and thrown shuriken. Another thing in this category is whips, which are a bitch to deal with, by the way.

The next group consists of fixed and flexible weapons. Both can be used real effectively against you in the hands of people who know what they're doing.

Fixed Weapons. Anything that stays the same shape when you use it: bats, bottles, pans, clubs, knives, tables, and these sort of things all qualify.

Flexible Weapons. These take a lot of practice with to be good for anything but a first strike. When you've gotten used to them, though, they can be really devastating. Since they're flexible, they can be either close range, distance, or projectile weapons. Look at a chain, for example. Wrap it around your knuckle for close range use, snake it out for long range use, or throw it around the legs of somebody who is running and it becomes a projectile. At the very least, they can be impact/trapping weapons. In this category there are whips, chains, ropes, nunchucks, yo-yos, monkey balls (basically a flail made out of rope), biker wallets, keys on chains, and belts.

These are some of the weapons you might encounter in an emergency situation. There are many others. What you have to do (unless you really like rude surprises) is take the basics I have told you about and go out and see how they apply to what's around you. A clam sheller in Maine will have different things around him to use than a roughneck in Texas. Those of you in the city have different options than those of you in the country (excuse me, ya'll in the country). Anyway you cut it, what you have to do is go out and try and see objects in a new way: what categories do they fall into?

The next step is to think about how you would use them in an actual emergency. This means defense, not offense. Not just how would you attack, but how would you defend with them? Surprise! A broken beer bottle is not a good defense against someone with a club. Especially if the guy has the smarts not to get too close. What are you going to do if he swings the club? Block with the bottle? Oh boy, that'd be interesting, wouldn't it?

That mentality leads into the third and most important step in your thought process. "How can these sorts of weapons be foiled?" Here is an important bit of advice—spend lots of time on this step. A major difference between me and some of these macho fuck martial art types who want to show nothing but attacks is that I don't like fighting. It's not some macho jock game to me. The reason is because where I'm from there was no such thing as a "friendly" fight. We went into it to hurt the fucker. This attitude led to some serious casualties. I'm talking not only wounds, but funerals. Those manly-man types have never really been on the receiving end of the shit. A week in the hospital and a month out of commission will put anybody's dick in line real quick.

This is where it's at with weapons. The other guy isn't going to stand there while you get ready to move—he's going to be throwing shit at you as fast as you're throwing it at him. This is why when dealing with weapons you must really know more about defense than offense. If you know how a weapon works, you know its strengths and weaknesses. This means you can prevent it from being fouled up in your hands, and yet, you can foul it up in other people's hands.

Now, boys and girls, comes the real goody. If you read my first book,[2] you'll know that I broke all the different types of blows into only four categories. This makes it real easy to get a grip on the basics. The goodie I was talking about is that the same thing can be done with weapons. *If you have an understanding of what is involved with the different basic weapon types, you can pick up damn near anything and use it to survive.*

The basics of quarterstaff/spear fighting apply to anything that you use in the same way. The basics of a yawara stick don't change because you're using a roll of dimes instead. All along the line, you discover this little point holds true. If you have a grasp of the basic weapon type, you'll know how to use whatever you end up grabbing at that moment. Zo' let uz take a louk at ze differen' weepon types! A hah hanh hanh!

---

[2] *Cheap Shots, Ambushes, and Other Lessons: A Down and Dirty Book on Streetfighting and Survival.* Paladin Press, Copyright 1989, ISBN 0-87364-496-4.

Quarter-staff, Polearm, and Spear

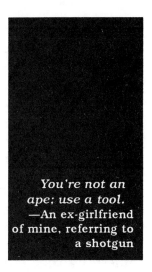

You're not an ape; use a tool.
—An ex-girlfriend of mine, referring to a shotgun

These three weapons are discussed together for one simple reason: many of the techniques are the same; yet, they're different enough to be confusing when you're reading about them. A lot of people think there isn't much difference, until they get taken out by a spear used as a quarterstaff or a quarterstaff used as a spear. Then they see the light. (You know, the white flash in your head when you get knocked on your ass.) So let's get into some hair splitting for a minute.

A big stick with nothing on the end is a quarterstaff. With this, you can pretend you're Robin Hood having it out with Little John. Quarterstaff techniques are, generally speaking, big circles requiring lots of room. It's still a distance weapon, but it's sort of a close distance weapon (if that makes any sense at all). For the record, though, a quarterstaff is purely an impact/bludgeon weapon. You pick one of these up to clobber someone, plain and simple.

Now we add on the bells and whistles. But, to keep it easy, we're going to keep them in simple categories. In truth these categories blend into each other

25

(hell, truth be told, it's more confused than body parts in an orgy), but we'll pretend they're separate. A spear is either a stick with a point or a stick with some sort of poker attached. They're distance point weapons that you jab or poke and just generally annoy folks with from far away. The technique is mostly tight circles, which makes it handy in tight places, like hallways and alleys.

Polearms are a curious species. They range from something that looks like someone duct-taped a bowie knife to a broom handle to something that looks like someone took a magnet on a stick and poked it into a pile of scrap metal. While they can be used to poke, for the most part, their moves consist of slashing or whacking. They're circular moves, but with strikes thrown in. The size of the circles are smaller than with quarterstaves, but larger than spear circles. Basic polearms are called bills, while the more complicated ax/hammer/ice pick/hook/spike/blade/prong kinds have as many different names as they have funny shapes. I'm just going to call them all polearms or bills. Technically spears are also polearms (which basically means a weapon on a stick), but I want to keep things simple for awhile.

A Historical Perspective

Throughout history, mankind has come up with all sorts of ways to poke somebody's ass without getting theirs too close. With a little imagination, they began to add all sorts of shit into Column B.

In Europe, they began to add things that sliced, diced, crushed, trapped, maimed, and mutilated. These started with simple pikes (basically fifteen-foot spears). They'd get about four

layers of guys pointing these at some idiot knight.
(Knights had a habit of charging in and hacking
up peasants. Getting close to a pike wall on a
horse was like volunteering to be a pin cushion.
This sort of put knightly dicks in line real quick.)
Then came halberds (basically an ax-spear
combo), bills (blades with either hooks, spikes, or
both for hooking, catching, and cutting off heads,
arms, legs, and other pieces of stupid keeniggits),
partisans (glorified spears with prongs to keep the
guy from getting stuck too far on your weapon),
hammers (yep, against a man in armor, a war
hammer was more effective than a single-handed
sword—not only did it dent the guy's helmet, but
the spike drove through and put a sizeable dent in
the dude's brain), and cul de sacs/man catchers
(basically spiked mousetraps that dug into the
guy so you could drag him off his horse, where
your waiting buddies would settle his hash right
quick).

In the Orient, they came up with some pretty
weird ones as well. Things like tiger forks (big three-
prong forks that they really did use to hunt tigers
with until they discovered they could hunt each
other with them just as well), naginatas (basically a
samurai sword somebody duct-taped to a broom
handle), hokos (a weird blend of spear and mitten;
the spear has a thumb-like blade that sticks out at
a ninety-degree angle—I swear, it looks mitten),
kumade (yes, the Japanese came up with a war
rake—no shit, it's a rake), and yawari (generic
Japanese name for spear, but they came up with
some weird ones—some of the things look like they
taped needle-nose pliers, shuriken, table forks, and
tin can lids onto spears).

In the West, we've lost most of the techniques

on how to fight with quarterstaves and spears. Our military decided it was easier just to shoot and bomb people. Great for them—they can afford planes to carry the bombs; I have to carry the fuckin' thing myself if I want to drop it on somebody (dealing with the blast radius is a bit of a bitch, too). So because the military has more money to spend on neat toys than I do, we're going to have to live with this lack of knowledge of the proper way to use a polearm.

Most of the formal knowledge we have concerning these fighting techniques comes from the Orient. In many cases, what is taught is too formal. If you have a spear- or bill-like weapon and somebody gets past your guard, you'd better know how to shift to quarterstaff technique pretty fuckin' quick.

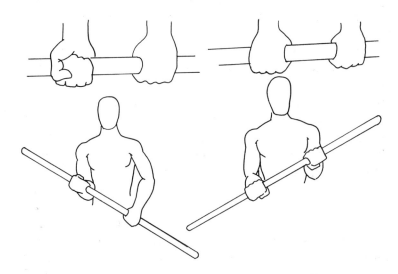

European and Oriental quarterstaff grips. European (left), with hands held in opposing directions. Oriental (right), with hands held in same way.

Grips

There are two basic grips you can use here. They have proper names, I'm sure, but ever since I got drunk and puked on a temple carving, I haven't really cared about being proper. I call them the Oriental and the European grips. These grips aren't exactly carved in granite; depending on the immediate need, they do switch back and forth.

I prefer a combination of the two, leaning to the European. The reason I like it is it makes it harder to knock the weapon out of your hand. This is something that happens a lot when you're fighting quarterstaff against quarterstaff. There's also a trick that you can do (which I'll explain later) that enables you to hit harder than you can with the Oriental grip.

The real thing to know about the European grip is that it is a distance grip, as in spear and polearm distance, which is three to six feet. In that range, it is an awesome force to contend with. If, however, the guy gets within three feet, you should consider shifting to the Oriental grip.

This is a new range called "near distance" (as big of a contradiction in terms as "military intelligence"). Anyway, near distance is close quarterstaff fighting, and here, the Oriental grip is the better choice. The reason for this is simple—in tight, the European grip sucks. What I mean by this is that depending on which hand is held up or down on the grip, one side of your blocks are going to be seriously klutzy. In case you don't know, *that would be bad.* The Oriental grip won't cross your arms up—in close, it's fast enough to deal with a rapidly shifting situation without tying you up like a pretzel.

However, the Oriental grip does have potential for a major glitch. If you're going to use it, you have to be more accurate with the angle of your blocks, or the impact will blast your weapon out of your hands.

Pivoting

A major aspect of quarterstaff fighting is pivoting. Most people try to move both hands when they try to block with a quarterstaff. You don't need to do that, nor do you really want to. The reason is it takes

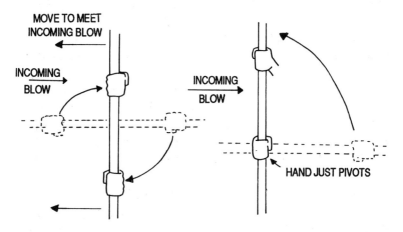

Pivoting. Model at left, in which both hands move, is not so hot. Shown at right is the preferred technique, wherein one hand remains stationary.

longer. With anything that takes longer, you run the risk of getting your head knocked into the next state. Take a look at what I mean. Basically, the hand on the side that the blow is coming into stays stationary. It's the other hand that does the moving.

Stances

Polearms work best in open spaces. A corridor about five feet wide and ten feet high is real friendly to imagine yourself working in. This gives your tip room to move. With quarterstaves, you need a hunk of space, like an empty parking lot, because unlike with polearms and spears, in quarterstaff fighting you use both ends of your staff to nail the sucker. You're swinging around a club of up to eight feet, so you kind of need to get the fine china out of the way. Spears need limited side-to-side space, but they're kind of persnickity about having backward and forward moving space. (Actually, the same applies to the polearm corridor—it, too, needs depth.) This is because spears are for thrusting and need less width for operating space.

If you find yourself in a limited space situation, you have to adjust your technique accordingly. This means you may have to use a

Note that both the quarterstaff (left) and polearm (right) stances are forward horse stances; just the torso and arm positions change.

quarterstaff like a spear. You may not be able to stab; however, the butt of a broom can knock the snot out of someone pretty good when used like a spear. Take a look at the difference between quarterstaff and polearm/spear stances and see why a hallway might interfere.

Blocking and Parrying

There are a couple of schools of thought regarding the number of blocking/parrying sectors (areas—defined by imaginary lines drawn around your body—within which blocks and parries work) in quarterstaff, spear, and polearm fighting. It ranges from four to fifteen. (By the way, the difference between a block and a parry is that a block stops a blow, while a parry deflects it. Either way, you don't get hit. I'll go into it more later.) The lower numbers apply more to basic blocks with quarterstaves, while the higher numbers include both blocks and parries and lean more to polearms. I personally vote for the ten-sector school as a happy medium, but only because I'm paranoid and I'm used to fighting people who know the sort of nasty things I do.

The Four-Sector School
The four-sector school is more suited for dealing with swinging attacks. That's why I said it's more for strict quarterstaff work, like if you're attacked by somebody who doesn't really know what he's doing. It's pretty simple in its breakdown: left side, right side, high guard, and low guard.

As you can see, these pretty well cover the sides, head, and nuts from wild swings. Now, pay attention to the type of grip being used in these draw-

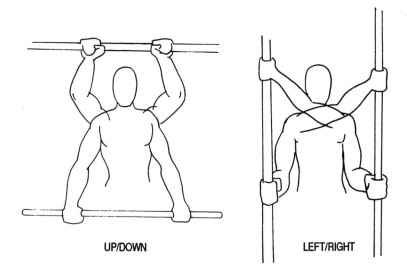

UP/DOWN LEFT/RIGHT

The four basic blocks of the four-sector school.

ings, because they are the best grips for getting into these blocking positions. Later, I'll point out where the grips get clunky.

The Six-Sector School

Now, other people break the four basic blocks down further into six sectors: high left, low left, high right, low right, high guard, and low guard.

These people like to block with the section that's in between their hands, because while you run the risk of getting your little paws whapped, you are also taking the hits on the most stable part of your weapon. A problem with the four-sector theory is if somebody hits near the end of the staff, the blend of impact and leverage can blow the weapon out of your hand. By using the six-sector defense, you can reduce the risk of that happening, but you must be more accurate with your hand placement.

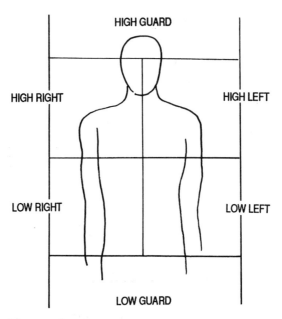

Six blocking sectors.

The Ten-Sector and Up Schools

The ten-sector theory deals not only with blocks, but parries also. This begins to bleed into polearm fighting. If you take the six-sector theory and add on these four parrying sectors, you get ten.

These are the four basic spear/polearm parries. Some people go into some fine differentiations at this point, dividing the four outer parrying sections (above) into nine sections—upper left, middle left, and lower left; upper middle, middle middle, and lower middle; and upper right, middle right, and lower right—which leads to the fifteen count. (It works, but I think it's just being persnickity over details. I just vary the size of parries to overlap. It's worked for me, but you may feel more comfortable with the fifteen, which is why I mention it.)

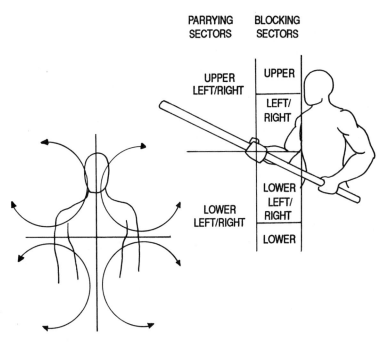

PARRYING SECTORS

BLOCKING SECTORS

UPPER LEFT/RIGHT

UPPER

LEFT/RIGHT

LOWER LEFT/RIGHT

LOWER LEFT/RIGHT

LOWER

The front and side views of the four outer parrying sectors.

Here, the four outer parrying sectors are divided further into nine sections.

The Right Way and the Wrong Way

As I said earlier, the difference between a block and a parry is that a block stops a blow, while a parry deflects it. For the most part, you use blocks to stop swings and parries to stop thrusts, although in a limited sense, they are interchangeable at times. In other words, they work on things they weren't supposed to work on sometimes. Unlike blocks, which are more crescent but terminate at a point, parries are pure circles. Whichever side you are protecting will determine which way you parry—clockwise or counterclockwise.

The reason the first one is considered correct is

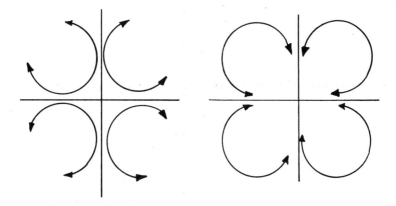

The parry shown at left is correct. If you parry inward, as shown at right, you risk allowing your opponent to get in and stab you on the right side. This wasn't the side he was aiming for, but nevertheless . . .

because parries done this way take the point of your opponent's weapon to the outside. This means the guy's weapon is no longer pointing at you; if it keeps coming, it's going to miss. If you parry inward, you run the risk of the guy still coming in. This means he stabs you on the right side of the chest rather than the left side he was aiming for. (I somehow doubt that he's going to stop and say it didn't count because that wasn't what he was aiming for, so when you practice these things, remember to deflect outward.)

Now I'm going to do a famous Animal flip-flop. You *can* parry the way I just told you not to. In fact, you should practice it. The truth is, every now and then you're going to have to do something downright stupid in a fight—things like parry inward, drop your weapon, turn your back on an opponent, leave a hole in your defenses, and so on. I keep telling people fights are unpredictable, but I can predict one thing about them—sooner or later, something straight out of left field is going to happen.

This is why you should know how to deal with inside parries. It's a case of understanding the odds: four out of five times, an inside parry will work to stop a thrust; it's that fifth time that's a bitch. Since you only get four shots, you had best be sparing about using them. If you're sloppy about using them all the time, when you really need it, it's going to be the fifth time. (Murphy's Law, not mine.)

What usually leads up to these sort of situations is the guy shifts positions on you or does something weird like a double lunge. Suddenly you find yourself—after doing a "right" move—with a point still heading for your gut. Okay, it's improvisation time. The way I deal with having to do something that I know is dangerous (like an inside parry) is to add mobility to the equation. Yes, I am doing an inside parry; I am also getting my ass out of the way.

A similar exception to the rule occurs with blocking a thrust. In general, parries are better for thrusts than blocks, just like blocks are better than parries for swings. The rule can be broken, though, and every

now and then you'll have to do it. This is the time to
remember how to side step. Often what this action
will lead to is a shift in the weapon use. If someone is
using spear/bill technique against you and they move
in such a way that you have to block rather than
parry, there is a good chance that they have moved
into quarterstaff range. This means you have the
opportunity to bean them, or you should be careful of
said attempts in your direction.

So by using these "wrong" moves sparingly and
throwing mobility into the equation when you use
them, you can greatly increase your chances of con-
tinued respiratory process (breathing).

Grip Improvisation

Now back to grip for a minute. Remember I told
you that while I preferred the European to the
Oriental grip, I used both? The thing is, both have
some serious boogers about 'em. In the drawings of
the defense sections, I showed you the grips in their
strongest blocks. The problems with these grips can
be broken down into two types: clumsiness and lack
of strength. This especially becomes apparent when
you are fighting with quarterstaves.

Defense

As I mentioned before, the European grip is
especially useful for polearm/spear fighting, due to
its flexibility. In quarterstaff fighting, however, there
are certain attack areas which either you take the
long way around to get to (this seriously increases
your chances of getting clobbered) or you end up
wrapping your arms up like a pretzel. This is what I
mean by clumsiness, something this grip is real
susceptible to. The areas of clumsiness depend on

which hand is held up or down. Take a look at the illustrations. The fastest pivots lead to crossing your arms, which you really don't want to do.

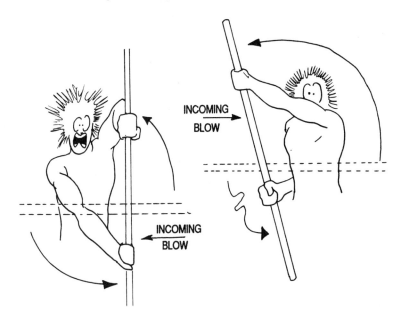

Clumsy sectors with the European grip.

If, instead of tying yourself into knots, you go for the long way around, you run the risk of two things. One is not getting there in time (painful). The second is not only painful, but downright embarrassing. Often you will scoop up your opponent's quarterstaff inside your defenses. This means not only are you getting hit by his energy, but you're adding yours to it. Why don't you just pick up a hammer and hit yourself and save the other guy the trouble? No shit, man, it happens this way. Look at the picture and you'll see how it can go down.

Fortunately for those of you who aren't into beat-

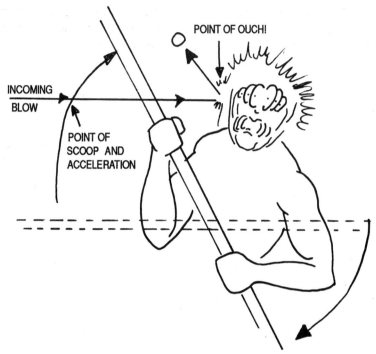

Physics involved with hitting yourself.

ing yourself up there's something you can do to prevent this from happening too often. Especially in the
areas where you run this risk, parry/strike outward
into the section that it's coming into. If you can hit his
quarterstaff near his hands (or his hand itself for that
matter) you can seriously foul him up sometimes.
That means try and keep it out in spear distance if
possible. This is why I go for the ten-sector defense
plan, you can reach out and touch someone right in
the kisser. If the guy gets too close, though, you might
want to consider shifting to the Oriental grip.

With the Oriental grip, if somebody whacks your
quarterstaff real hard, they can knock it out of your
hands real quick. This is the problem of the grip's

lack of strength. The only things keeping the weapon in your hands are your thumbs. In order to solve this dilemma, you have to block in certain ways. Unfortunately, your opponent probably isn't going to be polite and limit his attacks to suit your needs.

In a sense, the weakness of the Oriental grip is only on downward strikes. Yet, it is good against a downward strike aimed at your head if you do it right (we'll talk about that in a bit). Since not all downward strikes are going for your head, you have to watch yourself when you use this grip. As well as busting heads, downward strikes can bust knees, nuts, and shoulders. Another place where the weakness of this grip comes into play is with a double strike. Say someone strikes to your left side and you block. Up to this point it's fine; where it gets complicated is if the guy follows with a second strike to the right side. Unless you can shift your wrist position at the same time, the impact is going to where your thumbs meet up with your fingers, instead of to your arms. This is the same thing as a downward strike—it'll blow the weapon out of your hands. Take a look at the illustration below.

So if you're going to use the Oriental grip, you'll need to pay more attention to your wrist work to

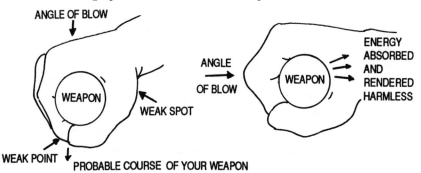

Thumb vs. wrist absorbing energy of blow.

prevent getting your weapon knocked out of your hand. One final point about the Oriental grip. I find it a little more limited in regard to polearm fighting. In fact, most Oriental forms that I know shift to the European grip when they use polearms.

One thing most people forget when they are quarterstaff fighting is that all parts of a quarterstaff can be used. That means not only can you swing and thrust, but you can (honest to god) punch. Most people will walk up to you when you're holding a pole and expect you to swing. What they don't expect is a double-arm punch that still uses the quarterstaff to knock their teeth down their throat.

Offense
Okay, I've rambled on enough about the defensive aspects of grips, let's get offensive! When it comes to attacks there are some things affected by the type of grip you choose. Little things like speed, strength, mobility, and adaptability, nothing really important. LIKE HELL! The grip you choose affects it all, folks.

The Oriental grip relies more on arm strength for striking. With the quarterstaff technique, you are punching short and letting the staff strike long. Quarterstaves are relatively slow when held in the Oriental grip (sort of like a .45 auto is slow to a 9mm, so don't be fooled).

One way of making quarterstaff strikes stronger and faster is this: as you're striking with one arm, pull back with the other. This puts the pivot point in the spot between your hands and increases power. If you don't do this, the hand that isn't striking becomes the pivot point. This can interfere with your strike if your timing isn't right. It can act as an anchor as well as a pivot, which is good for blocks but not so hot for strikes.

I like the European grip because even though it's sort of spastic on quarterstaff defense, it's a real mother on the offense. There are two variations of this grip—attack and defense. On the defense, you hold onto that quarterstaff for dear life. But when you're attacking, your hands should roam over that quarterstaff like it's a pretty and willin' woman. By loosening and then shifting your grip, you can change to anything from quarterstaff, spear, polearm, to a giant baseball bat. I mean this mother is flexible—and *fast.*

Now for the trick I mentioned earlier, when we first got into grips. It's called the whip technique. (Not bondage! Sheesh!) With the proper combo, you can turn your quarterstaff/polearm/spear into something like a giant fly swatter. It is mothering fast, harder hitting, and as unpredictable as a drunk Texan. You keep your leading hand loose (except for your thumb and forefinger, which you lock down nice and tight). This turns that hand into the pivot point for the whole operation. In the meantime, your rear hand is wiggling around like a snake on a hot plate. If you lead out into polearm form you get an off-balance hourglass effect. This means your rear hand moves three inches, but your polearm end moves three feet!

If you use this as a whipsaw technique, you can knock somebody's teeth loose in under a second. That's because all you had to do was move in an arc a total of six inches, while the impacting end moved a similar arc of six feet in the same time. Guess which one was moving faster and had more impact per square inch?

An important thing to know about any impact,

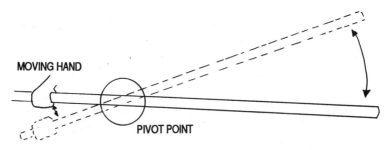

MOVING HAND

PIVOT POINT

Hourglass effect.

whether it be by hand or weapon, is depth. You want the end of your move to end about two inches into the guy. This means you stop your swing, poke, punch, strike, or kick two inches inside your opponent. That means instead of trying to blow a hole through the guy, you put all the energy somewhere between the front of him and the back of him. Most people throw strikes that hit the guy and try to push through him. *No, no, no!* When that happens the blow is interrupted before it can deliver all of its clout. The most energy is transferred at the terminal point of an action. This is why I can slap harder than most people can punch. Most people's punches when they hit are trying to push through the body. It hurts but doesn't do too much damage. A well-delivered blow is like having a brick wall slam into you.

With the whip technique you aim the end of whatever weapon you're using at your target, not on the other side of the guy. This delivers all the clout of the action rather than having it interrupted. This also allows mobility up the whazoo. Someone using this technique can strike not only anywhere, but multiple times. The tip is going too fast to watch (try to watch and you had better plan on taking up astrology—you're going to sit there and look at all the pretty stars).

The way to defend yourself against this sort of unpleasant shit is to ignore the tip and watch the center. You can't stop the end result, but you can pull the plug and stop the whole thing. This is also where you want to try to get your parries—while avoiding the same from happening to you. Fifty pounds of pressure at the center can translate to five hundred at the tip. If that tip gets near your center, you can lose your grip if it hits right.

Another thing you should know. When someone uses a polearm or quarterstaff as a bludgeon, get the fuck out of the way! Do not try to block, do not try to parry. Move! There is a good chance that he may only be using a pendulum effect, but that's still painful. You're in serious trouble if he knows what he's doing because he'll use both pendulum and whip technique. The same rules of physics that make up the whip technique apply here, but tenfold! How hard can you swing your arms? That's the center pressure. So you can guess what the force is at the end of a quarterstaff. If you can't get out, dodge, or duck, drop everything and rush the motherfucker. At the least, it'll reduce the damage. At best, you might avoid critical damage and get inside his guard. Quarterstaves suck in wrestling matches. If you try to take a blow from these swings, NORAD will be able to track your ass.

A Word About Bills

Now that you know something about technique, let's get into some specific details about polearm fighting, mainly bills. The bill started out as farm equipment, but ever since a shit-covered peasant picked it up and started whittling on a Viking, it's gone through some changes. Not only did the shape and size change, but they began to call it some weird names: guisarms, fauchards, Lochabar axes, couteaux de breche, Jedburgh axes, kumades, scythes, and a shitload of others.

I'm just going to call all of these things "bills." Incidently, this generalization is going to drive weapon historians and D&Ders batshit. These are the kind of people who will sit up all night and argue about whether the Lochabar axe was a Scottish weapon pre-1550 or post-1550. Or was it just another name for a bill, which would mean it had been around since the Dark Ages at least.

Let the historians argue semantics. What I mean by bill is basically a combination polearm that has the capability to trap. Whether it be hooked, spiked, or flanged doesn't matter to me. It's something that can be used to trap you in a fight. This is something that you have to watch out for.

The bitch about bills is that they are usually combinations of three or more items from Column B. The odds are you will initially be attacked with some other aspect of the bill than the trapping, the most common being point or impact, followed by edge and ripper. (Most people forget they can trap until way too late.)

Let's look at a shovel. Any shovel is a perfect example of what I mean by a bill, the most common being the spade and the scoop. Different areas can be used for different combos.

The spade can be used more as a spear (point/edge), but the scoop has more ripping capabilities as well as being an edge. Both have impact capabilities and trapping capabilities that come from the back flanges.

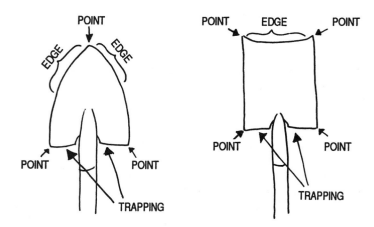

Shovels with key attack points.

If someone were to lunge past you, they could draw back and drive a ripper point into you. With that stuck in you all it takes is a shift of the person's body weight and you're on the ground, helpless.

So a major thing about bill weapons is you have to remember all the combinations they can be. They may not all get used, but any one of them could show up at any time. This is trickier than you'd think, and at the same time much easier. You have to practice and have experience with all aspects. If you only have this information in your head, you're dogmeat in a fight. If, however, you go out and spend a couple of days practicing all the aspects of fighting with a spade, then do the same with a scoop shovel, then a peat shovel, and so on, you're going to get this stuff ingrained. After that, go out and try rakes, pruning hooks, brooms (all those bristles are great rippers/points against delicate eye tissue), tikki torches, school window openers, mulchers, snow shovels, or anything else indigenous to your area or your place of work.

In time you'll begin to get the hang of how these things work. With that will come all sorts of knowledge as to what combinations come with different things. If you've practiced with whatever's laying around, you'll know what to watch for when somebody tries to nail you with it.

You need to take what you've learned here and go out and pick different things up and practice what we've been talking about. These are the general rules that can apply to any type of big stick you can pick up in an emergency, including shovels, rakes, brooms, standing lamps, and anything else that's handy.

You can also buy books on staff and spear fighting. What you know now will cover a lot of aspects those books don't. The thing is, all of the information in the world isn't going to do you a bit of good unless you practice it. So for sure, get the books, mock weapons, and a partner and practice this stuff before you really need it. Without a partner, drill with the real items that you might end up using. (I don't want to hear about somebody who got a shovel shoved into his chest by his buddy while dueling, so use practice weapons.)

You might want to check out various martial art schools in your neighborhood and see what they have to offer in the way of weapons training. There are certain Chinese forms that deal with weapons in depth. Most of the karate schools don't really get into weapons as deeply as they should. So this may be a dead end.

However, if you're into the slightly unusual social situation there is another real good alternative. There is an international organization called the "SOCIETY OF CREATIVE ANACHRONISM" (not anarchy—an anachronism is something still around but wildly out of date, like the electoral college). Their shortened common name is "The SCA." These people are in all major cities and are like termites. Unless you know what to look for, you'll never know they're there. They're a group of people who dress up in medieval clothes and socialize. They also put on armor and knock the shit out of each other with all sorts of "historical"-type practice weapons. This is actual hands-on experience with spears, polearms, and quarterstaves. If you're really interested in what this kind of fighting is about, this is the place to go. They have tournaments and everything.

I'm not a member, but I've known about them for a while. You can usually find them through gun shows, antique weapons dealers, science fiction circles, Renaissance fairs, college history departments, military miniature war gamers, and any reenactment-type group. If all else fails, they meet in parks for their tournaments, so look for signs saying "SCA" or people wandering around in medieval clothes.

Swords and Bludgeons

A lot of times, I'll go pick up the novelization of a movie I really like. One of my favorite movies is called *The Duelists*. Not only is it directed by Ridley Scott (one of my favorite directors) but it has William Hobbs (*Three* and *Four Musketeers* and *Ladyhawke*) as the fight choreographer. Beauty and the beast, man! The movie is the closest example of what weapons fighting is about—people getting hurt. It takes place during the Napoleonic Wars, when dueling was an acceptable way of settling disputes. If you were challenged, your "honor" said you had to fight the guy. Thing was, it had gotten to the point where if one of the guys was wounded, it was over. If the guy was down, you couldn't kill him. (There were people called "seconds" who would waste you if you broke this law.)

Well, into this loop is thrown a loonytoon. This guy keeps coming back for more. Because the duelists can never quite kill each other, this ends up going on for fifteen years. (It's a hell of a good movie; I highly recommend it.) Anyway, in one of the duels, one guy lunges and stabs the other guy in the chest.

51

The blade bounces off the rib (as they often do, especially if you don't hold the blade horizontal) and just fucks up the muscle. That's the end of that round. The guy's arm is out of commission. (All the muscles are interrelated. If you get stuck in the upper chest or shoulder it'll affect your arm. No shit). They go off and wait another five years and a few wars later to try and carve each other up.

What didn't come out in the movie so well but was mentioned in the book is that the guy who lunged led with (by all rules of fencing) the wrong foot! The other guy was taken totally flat-footed and got stuck because of it. It was the loonytoon who was doing the attacking, by the way, which is important to know because it shows he was so interested in sticking the other dude that he wasn't thinking about technique. Because he wasn't thinking, he did something totally outside the normal rules of fencing. It was so out of line it was unexpected. Because it was unexpected, it worked—*once*.

In a fight all it takes is that once. When most people pick up a weapon, they'll attack along certain lines. This is nice, because most of these lines are dealt with by certain types of training. That's the good news. The bad news is there are certain blind spots to training. If the person you're fighting either knows about these spots or accidently finds them, you're gonna be in a world of hurt.

As an example, there is a combo I know of in Shotokan karate that you can set your watch to. Fortunately, not too many people know about it. I'm not going to say what it is 'cause I use it to handle people who are better martial artists than I am. (There are a lot of people who fall into this category.) What you should remember is when these people start this combo, you let the first two moves slide by and then kick. I swear to God, they walk right into it almost every time.

The reason this kind of thing happens is that formal styles lull people into dealing with certain types of situations in certain ways. One way of looking at it is it's like a huge chunk of land with roads on it. Some of the roads are paved and some aren't; in other spots there ain't no road at all. Certain vehicles have been adapted to run on- or off-road. Some on-road vehicles have turned into specialized beasts that can do incredible things, but only on the road. While there are slower, more adaptable vehicles rolling around that operate on both paved and unpaved roads, there are others that are simply off-road monsters. These suckers should have SS *ENTERPRISE* painted on the side: "to boldly go where no man has gone before." But because of their specialization, they have certain limitations. It's this little fact that most people forget when they get into training. You wouldn't expect a 4 x 4 to win a road race against a Formula One race car, would you? Nor would you expect a Formula One race car to do so well crossing a river bed. Then why in God's name do people expect karate to cover everything that they might encounter? Let me say right now, karate is a Japanese pickup truck! Kendo is a sedan! Judo is a rice grinder motorcycle! *Don't expect them to handle everything!* Most barroom brawlers are these huge 4 x 4 one-ton pickups that run over anything that gets in their way. Western fencing techniques are V-8 dual carb monsters. Wrestlers are Harleys. If you meet any of these things on their own turf, you're in some shit. Savvy?

The reason that I tell you this is you need to know what you're up against and where you are.

With this information, you can know whether to stay put, get the hell out of there, or alter the situation. While this is true of fighting in general, it is wildly true in the area of stick/sword fighting.

There's a thunder'n herd of fighting forms for sticks, clubs, and swords. The reason I combine all of these weapons in one chapter is that the techniques can be smudged together in many ways.

Now, you can pick up a club and haul off and hit somebody with it. Maybe you can keep from getting hit by something by blocking with that same club. It works—sometimes. There's a good chance, though, that something will go wrong and you'll never know what it was 'cause you're laying on the floor taking a little nap.

History and Background

With a little work and research, you can become a devastating whirlwind of attacks, strikes, counters, parries, and blocks with damn near any club-like item you pick up. Believe it or not, clubs are the easiest and most available improvised weapons to learn how to use.

Aside from various stick fighting techniques, there is a wide variety of sword training available. Some of the stick fighting techniques are in kali/escrima, pananandata, choy le fut gung fu, and Okinawan karate. The Filipinos have some of the most defined forms for stick fighting in the world, and these bear looking into. In the sword fighting arena, you have Western fencing (using three types of weapons), kendo, iado, ninjutsu, broadsword and shield, all sorts of Chinese styles (no shit, almost every style of gung fu has sword technique in it somewhere), and a Hindu style (the name of which escapes me).

Any one of these can put a dent in your hat pretty damn quick. One of the easiest and most accessible to find is Western fencing, though, and this is what I recommend. I have formal training in fencing and informal training in broadsword and kendo. I have fought kali/escrima and practiced against it as well. In practice only, I have gone up against Okinawan and Iado. I have *seen* Hindu and Shao Lin forms in action. But in my opinion, the best way to learn basic stick fighting technique is through Western fencing. It's easy to learn and it's a bitch to get around. The three types of weapons—foil, épée, and sabre—will cover damn near every basic approach you'll encounter. The weapons you learn with are watered-down versions, but if you practice with heavier objects you'll be able to chaff out the stuff that has crept in with the use of toy swords. (By the way, I may joke about "toy swords," but I have bled because of those damn things. It's actually similar to fighting with a car antenna. They may be light, but until you've been slashed with either a car antenna or a sabre you have no idea how much they can hurt.)

My next choice is the Filipino styles. There's a good, practical reason for this. For centuries, the Philippines were the crossroads of the East and West. Anybody who did trade in the Orient used the Philippines as a gas station. Also, the Philippines are a great strategic point in military terms, so everybody and their brother sent their soldiers through.

Because the islands are such a crossroads, the Filipino fighting styles reflect Eastern martial arts and Western sword fighting, as well as all the nasty shit that five hundred years of soldiers and sailors can come up with. Believe me, that's a lot. Think about it. There you are, merrily carving each other up using your basic techniques. One day, a big boat shows up. "Great! Let's go carve these white assholes up." *Boom,* you meet a cannon for the first time. *Ouch.* "Okay, maybe you guys can stay." The whites hang around, get drunk, and fight a lot. Your home is now a "port o' call." Your old techniques were pretty good, even if they couldn't stop a cannon. Let's just mix them in with some of these things the white men do and see what we get. (After all, not too many drunks carry a cannon when bar hopping.) "Hey, this works!" Five hundred years of making money off the honkies and knocking heads with 'em and the Filipinos came up with some practical fighting techniques.

Next, I recommend the Oriental sword techniques, with kendo at the bottom of the list. There's a reason for this. The popularity of kendo, like Bruce Lee, is mostly a media invention. One thing most people don't realize is Japan is one of the few countries that kicked the world out and went back to the old ways. In the sixteenth century, Portugal made contact with Japan. Then under the Tokagawa Shoganate they kicked the West out. I mean "Fuck You," "Closed," "Gone Fishing," "Keep Out," "No Trespassing." Kicked out. They legislated guns and went back to the sword. Then, in 1853, Commander Perry sailed into Yedo Bay, shoved a cannon down their throats and said, "Hi there." Thus ended Japan's closed door policy.

This created a market for Japanese art, trade goods, and philosophy (does this sound familiar?) in the early 1900s. It also introduced fighting forms that hadn't had to adapt to the reality of changing circumstances (like guns and the average white Joe being able to slit your throat). But because of its "purity," it was a big splash.

Let's take a look at it though. In Japan, you had the samurai and the feudal systems. Because it was—and still is—an island, and it's on the far side of everything, Japan has never really had to deal with a strong invading hostile force. (I'm not counting World War II; that was aided and abetted by guns.) The Mongols tried in the thirteenth century. The first bout was an inconclusive battle on the shore (landings are a bit of a bitch) and the second time the fleet got creamed by a typhoon, the Divine Wind that protects Japan, the Kamikaze. Those few folks who didn't drown and got to the shore were butchered by the samurai. That was the only time Japan was attacked by a sword-wielding world in nearly a thousand years.

The Japanese did, however, make forays into Korea in the Middle Ages. The territory they seized they didn't hold for long. The Chinese and Koreans eventually kicked them out. This should really tell you something about the Japanese fighting techniques versus other systems. Basically, the Japanese, kept their system going because they were off the beaten path. Meanwhile, everybody else was busy fighting off the fucking savages from the Asian steppes. (The names changed—the Shang, the Huns, the Mongols, the Tartars, and finally, the Manchurians—but they were still nomadic barbarians who rode into town and raised hell. These guys were trouble. If they weren't herding horses, they were drunk. If they weren't drunk, they were fighting. If they weren't fighting each other, they were invading the world.)

Because of its closed door policy, Japan developed a self-contained group of fighting systems. The weaknesses of these techniques weren't weeded out because they were protected by tradition and culture. One of the biggies that most people forget with all their talk of Bushido is this little theory that the ultimate act of a samurai was to die in the service of his lord. On top of this glorified suicide attempt was the "double strike," where two samurai opponents kill each other at the exact same time. (Attack, don't defend.) They both struck each other down in a steel blaze of glory (or gory) in the name of Bushido. It proved that you were both of equal talent. Yeah, right. What it meant was you were both dead! This was built into the system!

Along with this was the fact that the samurai were macho gods protected both by the law and their swords (which only they could carry . . . it's easy to be tough when the other guy doesn't have a sword). The Okinawans and the ninja were the only ones coming up with different ways of dealing with these asshole samurai. I mean, here's a little peasant fisherman minding his own business and a samurai comes by and demands his catch. (According to the samurai, it's his right to take it.) "Hey, fuck you, pal. If I give you this catch my family doesn't eat." Samurai goes for his sword, and the fisherman, in total disregard of all rules of Bushido, sticks him with a fishing gaff, ties some rocks around the legs of the corpse and the samurai is fish food. This is how it worked in Okinawa and Japan for the average Joe (who, by the way, constituted about 80 percent of the population).

I'm not cutting down the fighting styles of Japan here. What I'm trying to do is point out that they are specialized. All sorts of people know about kendo. What few people know is when you put a kendoist against a fencer—or a broadsword and shield man for that matter—it doesn't come out the way T.V. makes you think it would.

God's truth, I once went up against a kendoist with sabre technique while drinking a beer. I had to put down the beer to finish him off, but I held him off with it in my hand. (I have to admit, I had seen the same thing in a Danny Kaye movie and wanted to see if it could be done). I was also at my fighting peak at the time, so that helped a lot. The thing is, kendo and iado have some damn good moves in them that you'd better have encountered on the practice mat beforehand or it'll get ugly.

Okay, there's been a reason why I've bored the shit out of you (and probably annoyed the shit out of some folk) with all of this. It's to give you some idea of where to go and what to watch for to learn about this sort of stuff. The reason is simple: WITH STICK FIGHTING YOU HAVE TO HAVE YOUR SHIT WIRED TIGHT! THIS IS AN AREA WHERE IT GOES DOWN HARD AND FAST! This isn't play time. This is where you will encounter most types of improvised weapons. So you had better do some serious studying in this field. Now, I've babbled on enough about history, form, and where you can go to perfect this stuff. Let's get on to the ass-kicking part.

Due to my training, a lot of what I'm going to show you here is fencing (with other stuff thrown in). I'll call everything a stick, rather than interchange bludgeon, sword, club, bokin, sabre, and teeth-knocker-inner. Let's look at grips first.

Grips

In stick fighting, you have the same three basic grips as in knife fighting (and a few others as well—we'll get to those later). These are the sabre, natural (or hammer), and Oriental (or ice pick).

Each has its place and uses, and the only time one is better than any other is on its own turf. If you try and fence with an Oriental grip, it's lousy. If you try to in-fight with a sabre grip, it's downright pathetic.

The sabre grip is the most flexible of the three. It's fast, and it relies on wrist work and strength.

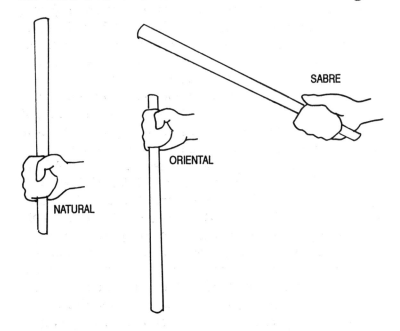

Here are the three main grips used in stick fighting.

Aside from speed and mobility, its other strength is that you can whip/snap by flicking your wrist. Its weakness is that your weapon can be knocked out of your hand easily. It is mostly designed to keep people at the farthest reaches of the stick's range.

The natural grip is less flexible and relies more on arm strength to get the message across. You use wrist work, but it's more of a pivot than a snap. This grip's big strength is that the weapon sits like the

Rock of Gibraltar in your hand and isn't going anywhere you don't want it to. Its weakness is that you sacrifice speed and mobility for a more solid grip. It's more for mid-range fighting.

The Oriental grip is a sleeper. It is definitely less flexible than the other two, takes more practice, and uses arm strength in some weird ways. It is also designed for fighting in close with sticks and will knock the shit out of anyone dumb enough to rush it. It is a blend between stick fighting and punching. If the guy can move his arm, he can use it against you. It's especially strong on defense. If you're being attacked by stick-wielding midgets, this is the grip to use. It can keep your lower sections intact. To block with it in the upper sections, just raise your arms. Most people don't think about stabbing with a stick, but with a flick of the wrist and a quick stab,

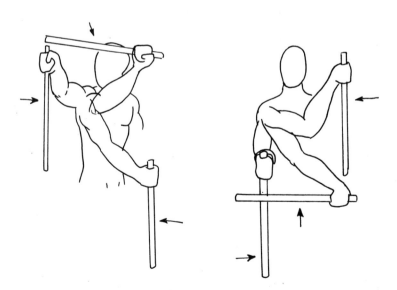

Blocking with the Oriental grip.

you could dent somebody's forehead. Most strikes are concerned with flicking your wrist, though. Especially with this grip, watch your nuts and knees from a ground position. The nice thing about this grip is that it looks like you're just standing there holding something like a cane.

Now for the other grips. If you were paying attention, you would have noticed that the natural and Oriental grips use the same hand positions; what changes is the placement of the hand on the stick. Same with the next grip, but the hand is either in the middle of the stick or a little closer to one end. I have no idea what this grip is called, so we have to make up a name for it until either I find out what the damn thing is called or you find the proper name in your travels and write me about it.

Um . . . let's call it the "bureaucrat grip." Yeah! 'Cause it looks like somebody whacking off! That describes most bureaucracies I know of. This grip is

Bureaucrat grip.

actually a good middle-of-the-line starting position. While it has some serious limitations as to flexibility and distance strikes, it has nice parrying abilities and some good middle- to close-range strike options. I'd advise shifting to something else if you want long-range results, however.

Unlike other grips, this one is mostly limited to circular moves. One of the nicest things about it is it doesn't look threatening. (See, I told you this was a good name for this grip. It's middle-of-the-road. It's only sort of flexible. Its strongest use is covering its own ass, it's nigh onto useless outside of its territory, it goes in circles, and it looks harmless unless you know what is really going on. The bureaucrat grip, hah! I calls 'em as I sees 'em).

Actually this isn't such a spazo grip as its name implies. It's one that will buy you time until you get into something else. Or, if you're not at all interested in counterattacking, just keep using it. Its one main weakness is against thrusts, though, but you know why that is so. Most moves are faster if your arm moves in circles rather than straight lines. This is true of most circular forms, because they don't have to start, stop, and start again, which straight lines do.

The bureaucrat is a great grip for a ready position. Often you'll find yourself in places where you're not sure which way the scales'll tip, violence or not. In these sorts of situations, any overt move on your part might be the deciding factor that tips things toward violence. Remaining calm is one of the best ways to keep things from getting violent. Knowing your ass is covered is a great aid to remaining calm, if you know what I mean.

Okay, let's look at the kendo grip. A kendo grip is *not* a baseball grip! It's more flexible. Remember

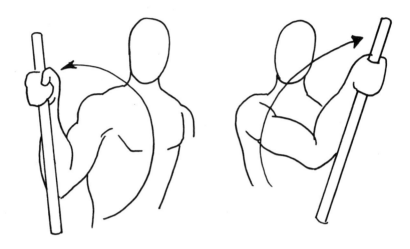

Blocking with the bureaucrat grip.

the whip technique I told you about in the last chapter? The one where the leading hand is held loosely except the thumb and forefinger, while the back hand is held tight? I'm going to call that the kendo grip, because that's where I learned it.

The absolute best part of this grip is it's great for the offense! I mean, it is a head knocker extraordinaire! The double grip of this and the baseball grip give you the most strike strength available. But there's one slight catch: defense. For blocks at the navel level and up, it's still hot. It's the part about covering your nuts that gets a little thin. Lower body parries and blocks take a long time to perfect. Because it was considered beneath the dignity of a samurai to kill with the point of his sword, kendo relies more on blocks than parries. This is why fencing works so well against it.

By the way, when I talk about this stuff, I'm talking to the average student. In America, a guy

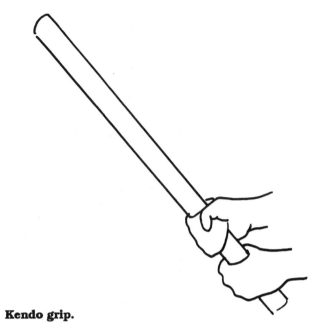

Kendo grip.

who has five years of study is usually awarded his black belt. Five years of martial arts training is not the same thing as devoting your entire life to it, which is what it takes to be a Master. I'm sure that one of these guys could make me a liar by proving on a mat that everything I say is wrong. Against them, that's true, but it's the students that'll get the shit knocked out of them by the sort of problems I'm talking about. I'm not talking to Masters here, I'm talking to you—what you have to contend with when the shit gets ugly. It's not a dojo out there. Unless he's trained, the guy's attacks aren't going to conform to a particular style. If he is trained, who knows what style it's in? All in all, this means that in a street situation you have to know how to deal with all sorts of wild and weird shit, as well as the unexpected. This is stuff they either never teach you or they gloss over, which is why the average martial artist loses in a real fight!

One of the things that never ceases to amaze me is the number of teachers who have never had to actually use their martial arts to defend themselves. They don't know what it really takes. They talk the talk, but they don't walk the walk. I was at a party once with a guy who was "a renowned martial artist." We're sitting there talking theory, and the guy says, "If I ever had to use this in an actual fight, I'd. . . ." I don't remember what the rest of the sentence was because when he said that I stopped in confusion and looked at him. (I tell you, I was seriously confused. Enough so that I stopped my beer halfway to my lips. We're talking big-time confusion. Normally, nothing gets between me, my beer, my woman, or my food.) I asked him if I had heard right. He looked at me and said "Yeah. Why, have you ever . . . ?" My response of "all the time" sorta shut down the conversation.

Anyway I've yapped enough. Another option would be to use quarterstaff grips, especially for blocks. While you can punch and jab with these grips, for strikes it's advisable to shift to another type of grip. From this it's easy either to drop into a double-handed attacking grip (kendo/baseball) or a single-hand strike.

The blocking technique is exactly the same as with a quarterstaff. You catch the impact between your hands. This is especially advisable to use if your opponent has something real heavy (like a car jack) that will knock your weapon out of your hand if it hits anything above your stick pivot point (explained later).

The baseball grip is what most people will do instinctively when they grab a stick. Just as the quarterstaff grip is almost purely defensive, this is

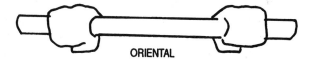

ORIENTAL

EUROPEAN

Quarterstaff grips.

Baseball grip.

usually almost always purely offensive. There's a reason for this, and it has to do with the physics of stick fighting. If you modify it by knowing these physics, it improves, but it still has the same problems as the kendo grip. Its one serious advantage is the sheer muscle you can put into a swing.

Swings

Speaking of swings, there are three ways to hit—strength, whip, and a combo of the two. The last one is the most devastating. Strength is real easy to explain—you just hit the guy with something. You swing your arm, it connects, end of story. This is used either by people who are totally unaware of whip or people who have something real heavy and hard to swing (like a car jack). Whip is a little harder to explain technique-wise. Basically, it consists of snapping your wrist in whatever direction you want to hit. It can be done from different angles (sometimes even different directions, like backwards, but that's a little tricky). For these snap/whip techniques, the sabre grip is the absolute best grip, but other grips will work, too. Take the stick and hold it in your hand, point up. Without bending your arm too much, bring the tip back to your shoulder. Now snap your wrist forward. Try this against a tree or something to see how hard you can hit with this. Do this at different strike angles until you get good. This is for lighter weapons that can be moved or for people who have wrists that would give a gorilla an inferiority complex.

The third type is a combo of the two. It consists of swinging your arms and snapping your

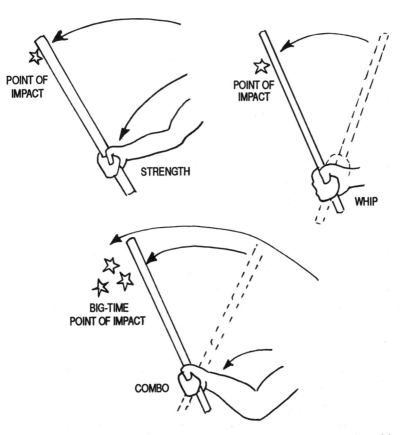

POINT OF
IMPACT

STRENGTH

POINT OF
IMPACT

WHIP

BIG-TIME
POINT OF IMPACT

COMBO

Shown here are the three types of strikes—strength, whip, and combination or terminal point.

wrist so it all comes together at once. Nighty-nite time. (No shit, if you get good at this combo you can knock people into tomorrow.) The timing on this one takes a little practice to perfect but is well worth it. You must practice until the swing (arc) of your arm terminates at the same time that the arc of the snap ends. When you have this right, not only does the impact of your arm strength hit the guy, it is multiplied by the impact strength of the whip.

Physics

Alright folks, it's time to put on your graduation caps. You're all going to become physics majors here for a bit. (Don't worry, it's not going to deal with math. You could probably figure out the math if you wanted to, but I'll just give you a situation and let you decide how far you want to take it. The story I'm going to to share with you will demonstrate how important the laws of physics are.)

A couple of years ago I was teaching sword fighting to the group of drunken perverts I hang out with. I had given them the basic drills and told them how to hold their wrists during each; it was time for the dull part of doing the techniques over and over again. There was a kid named Ron who was bored and whining, "Why do I have to drill?" I put up with it for a while, telling him that the moves had to become instinctive, which meant not only getting the sword there in time but in the right position and angle. He didn't exactly buy that. He felt he did have the moves down to instinctive memory and that he was ready for his first sword fight.

Anyway, Ron kept pestering me to let him fight. I kept telling him to drill. I could see by his drilling that he wasn't ready, but finally I said, "Fuck it. Come on. You want to fight? Fight me." This was a major source of amusement for the rest of the group, who knew what I could do. They all stopped what they were doing and grabbed their booze and women and settled down to watch with lopsided drunken grins.

Ron stood there for a second not sure what to do. (Up to this point it had always been one attacks, one defends, then switch off.) I settled the matter for him. The next thing this kid knew, I was all over him. He started backpedaling on the first swing and that's all he ever did. I took five swings and drove him back twenty feet. On the fifth swing, it happened. Ron managed to get the sword in the right place, but not in the right way. He blocked with the flat of the blade and his sword broke. My blow had chopped his sword off at the hilt (we still have it). Ron literally stopped and stared at the hilt. In the meantime, I was bringing eight pounds of broad sword to a screeching halt before I chopped him in half.

I looked at him and snarled, "Wrong move! Instead of looking at it you should have shoved that hilt down my throat!" He looked at me in total shock. After that he drilled without complaint.

It has taken you longer to read about what happened than it took for the actual event to go down. The elapsed time of that whole incident was about five seconds. That's how quick this shit is.

The point is that the major mistake that kid made was in the area of physics. That is why his sword broke and mine didn't. You have to be aware of how impacts affect the wrists, your weapon, and pivot points in stick fighting. This is what fucks most people up—they have no idea of what's involved and why. Anybody who is dumb enough to go after a fencer with a stick is going to learn real fuckin' fast how major this stuff is.

Effect on Grip

Okay, the first thing we're going to look at is how impact affects your wrist and grip. *If you don't shift your grip to meet the impact head on, you're either going to get your weapon knocked out of your hand or you're going to suffer wrist damage!* It is this important! Take a look at the following illustration.

The first hand is in a shitty position. The force of the incoming blow is going to knock the stick out of the fingers/thumb junction and/or knock the wrist inward. (The latter sort of impact causes damage and numbing, which slows down the body.)

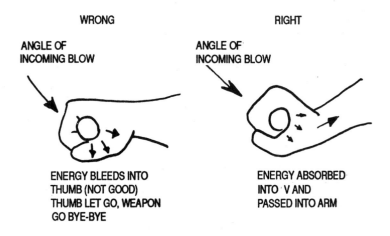

WRONG

RIGHT

ANGLE OF
INCOMING BLOW

ANGLE OF
INCOMING BLOW

ENERGY BLEEDS INTO
THUMB (NOT GOOD)
THUMB LET GO, WEAPON
GO BYE-BYE

ENERGY ABSORBED
INTO V AND
PASSED INTO ARM

Two hands, natural grip, one with wrist turned out, one with wrist turned in to receive outside impact.

The second hand is in a much better position believe it or not. The incoming force is deflected through the wrist and into the arm which acts as a shock absorber. The deflection starts the energy loss and the elbow and shoulder deal with the rest. Because the blow is being met head on, the stick is shoved back into the V of the hand and the palm. (In other words, it knocks it further into your grip, instead of out of it.)

The same thing goes for blows coming from the other direction. If your wrist is knocked loose, it starts the stick rolling out towards your fingers and eventually out of your hand. That's because it's your thumb that gives your hand holding strength.

The only time your hand should be held in a straightforward position is to take a straight incoming blow. Otherwise, you should adjust your wrist to take the impact directly into the V of your hand.

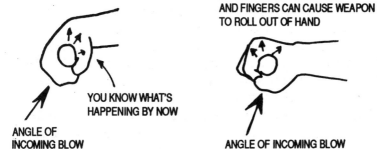

RIGHT

ANGLE OF
INCOMING BLOW

YOU KNOW WHAT'S
HAPPENING BY NOW

WRONG

ENERGY BLEEDS INTO PALM
AND FINGERS CAN CAUSE WEAPON
TO ROLL OUT OF HAND

ANGLE OF INCOMING BLOW

Wrist positions for receiving inside impact.

It doesn't matter which grip you use, this applies to them all. The basic physics of fighting is what causes this situation, and it transcends all styles, techniques, and forms. When you pick up a stick, this is the first thing you should learn.

Effect on Weapon

The second aspect of physics relates to your weapon rather than your grip. The reason Ron's sword broke was that he presented the weakest side to take the blow. This is something not too many people are conversant about. What the fuck will break your weapon? Which is the stronger side? You need to know this. Stop and think, which side of a 2 x 4 can you walk on safely? (Hint, the wrong answer is the lower number.) Why? Which side would you want to use to cover your ass? Makes sense when you look at it that way, doesn't it?

That is why it is important to block with the strongest side of your improvised weapon. This is something that you won't learn practicing shinai (bamboo-slat practice swords). This is because the shinai are round. There's a string to indicate the back, but in a practice bout, most people totally disregard that string (thereby all the physics of reality) and wail away at one another with any part of the sword. It's all speed, but no form. You had better damn well know the form if you pick up a 2 x 4 to fight a guy holding a length of pipe, because if you block wrong, the 2 x 4 will break.

Closely related to this is mass/velocity vs. breaking strength. Breaking strength refers to how easily something breaks or snaps. As an example, let's look at wood. The two kinds of wood that concern us here are hard wood and soft wood. Pine is soft, while oak is hard. A one-inch dowel of pine will break more easily than a one-inch dowel of oak, because the pine has a lower breaking strength. If you were to swing a one-inch diameter piece of lead pipe at it, the pine would snap, while the one inch oak dowel wouldn't. However, a two-inch dowel of pine might be able to compensate for the breaking strength difference.

While some things will smash other things, some things are faster. This is because of something called *momentum*. Momentum is a combo (product) of weight (mass) and speed (velocity). If you want to get technical about it, $M = m \times v$. There's a trade-off here. With the same amount of energy, lighter things (m) will move faster (v) than heavier things.

However, heavier things moving at the same speed as the lighter things take more energy to get to that point. This means they have a higher momentum. So even though it's traveling at the same speed, the heavier object is going to do more damage. It takes different energy levels to get things going. Lighter thing are faster on the draw, but heavier things do more damage when they hit.

I used to carry a light cane, no problem. With it I could take out much of what I was likely to encounter—chains, knives, nunchucks, and pool cues (all of them light mass). Then one day a guy came after me swinging a car jack. No way. It would've snapped the cane like a toothpick. Had I been cornered, my only option would have been to parry in hopes of deflecting his swings (not too likely). Attempting to block would have been suicide. Fortunately, I wasn't cornered and I ran like a motherfucker.

Another aspect of all this was that he came at me swinging. That meant he had gotten past the start-up stage, which is where the time is lost. Let's look at that a moment. It's a real compromise, speed vs. clout. A lighter weapon is faster off the starting line. It takes less energy. That means (usually) before the heavier weapon can get into motion the lighter weapon has struck. On the other hand, if the heavier weapon is already moving, the lighter weapon won't be able to stand against it. It's exactly like a rice grinder against a Harley. The rice grinder can jackrabbit off the starting line much faster than the hog. But if they meet on the open road where the Harley can unwind, it's a different story altogether.

An easy way to look at it is, offensively, a light weapon can strike faster, a heavy one harder. Defensively, the light weapon can't stop a heavy one; a heavy weapon might be able to get there in time to stop a light one.

Let us pretend that breaking strength doesn't exist (sort of like pretending taxes don't exist). In order to stop something dead in the water, you need to meet it with equal momentum. Like two cars of the same make going the same speed and hitting exactly head-on will stop dead at the point of impact (theoretically).

Now, what if the weights differ? Uh oh. We take two items of different weight and swing them at each other. One weighs three pounds and one weighs six pounds. In order to match momentum, the speeds would have to differ. A three pound weight going six feet per second would have equal momentum of a six-pound weight going three feet per second (3 x 6 = 6 x 3 = 18, for you visual folk).

What if they were traveling at the same speed? 3 x 3 = 9, 3 x 6 = 18. Guess who's going to need dentures? (Hint, bigger number wins.)

Unless the lighter one is moving fast enough to compensate for the weight difference, it has no chance of surviving. That was nice and pretty, but also unrealistic. Realistic throws in breaking strength, and God knows where that's going to lead you.

Your attitude has to reflect the weapon you have at your disposal. If you are using a cane against a jack, you have to start the show because if he gets moving, you're dog meat. If you've got the jack, you have to build up speed before the guy moves, otherwise you'll never make it. This means you have to watch yourself at all times. If you have a honker of a weapon that you have to get moving, you don't want anybody to get close to you until it's moving. If you've got a light weapon, you have to get it over quick or you're gonna be history.

Understand that the odds are you'll never meet toe-to-toe with somebody on equal improvised weapon levels. The only way I can think of is if you're in an area where multiple objects of the same sort are around, like at a pool hall, at work, or something like that. Usually, you have to grab what's around. Sometimes this means luck of the draw. If you get the club and he gets the chair, that's how it goes. It may be reversed. Or in an open situation, he gets the club and you get a bottle, in which case throw it at him and get the hell out of there, 'cause you're outmatched. This is real shit here. I'm not telling funny stories or spinning a long yarn about the history of something now. I do that to lighten it up and to get my point across sometimes, but this is serious nuts and bolts that you must know to keep from bleeding. Most of what's involved is knowing these things—the rest is just practice.

I don't know what sort of things you have around you right now that could be used as clubs, but you do. Look around and see what you'd use to hold off an attacker in this manner. From now on, when you walk into a place, scope out what you could use to defend yourself. Pick things up and start whapping them against other things. This will teach you how to feel breaking strength. Start looking for the different sorts of weapons I'm talking about in this book. The hardest part is turning on this awareness initially. After a few weeks, it becomes almost reflexive. Start picking things up and looking at them from the standpoint of how you would use them to defend yourself. You already have the three main categories you need to know: range (close, distance, thrown), type (edged, impact, ripper, etc.), and construction (fixed, flexible). Every weapon form I've talked about or will talk about falls somewhere within these categories. With the basics under your belt, you can use anything short of Jello as a weapon (and that you could use as a diversion, which we'll deal with later).

By going out and looking at these things in this light, you will begin to get a feel for what will or will not work, what sort of impact it will or won't take, and a whole host of shit that I could spend hundreds of pages explaining, but you'd still have to learn yourself anyway. I can't explain a feeling, which is what most of this stuff is.

Effect on Pivot Points

Another aspect of sword and stick fighting is pivot points. You have to consider both the raw weight of the object and the balance. The physical aspects of weight, balance, and pivot points are closely related to grips.

If something weighs three pounds, that's fine and dandy. But how is the weight distributed? There is a thing called "point-heavy," which means that a major portion of the weight is distributed at the front of the weapon. This will affect how you use the weapon. Lots of fighting forms are dependent on a certain type of weapon, many of which are point-heavy. A point-heavy weapon handles differently than a butt-heavy one. You should know how to handle both, because you never know what you're going to end up grabbing.

The best example of a point-heavy weapon is a hammer. All the weight lies at the opposite end of where you grip it. Yet, you swing it so that your hand is the pivot point.

If you have a gaff, the pivot point moves out onto

the handle; usually just in front of the handle. This is because it's longer, and therefore it's faster to have gravity do the work for you.

On certain point-heavy swords, the pivot point moves out into the center of the blade. These are unique swords, but they have a lot in common with certain types of tools you may have to grab.

There are other weapons where the weight is distributed evenly. The location of the pivot point depends on what fighting style you're using and the length of your stick.

If the bulk of the weight of the weapon is in the butt, the pivot point will almost always shift either into your hand or just in front of it. That's because you have the weight and the leverage right there. If, however, the weight is at the tip, the pivot point can shift into the center of the weapon. The reason for this is that sometimes it's easier and faster if your hand isn't the pivot point.

The easiest way to say this is that the pivot point becomes a spin point. Ever take a stick and spin it in the air in front of you? It sort of spins there for a second before falling down. Same thing. By moving the pivot point out onto the stick, you can speed up the whole process by whipping your hand up in an arc. If you try to use your hand as the pivot point, you're starting from a standstill, and you're using pure muscle to get the weight going. If, however, you move further out onto the stick, you're adding leverage and gravity to your muscle. It's the same thing with the hourglass leverage effect of quarterstaves. You only move your hand six inches, but the tip moves six feet. The sucker wants to go down because of gravity, but instead of shoving the tip over, you knock the stand out from underneath it. It takes less time, muscle,

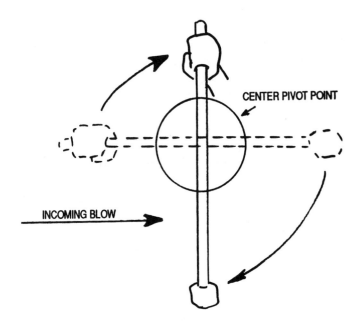

CENTER PIVOT POINT

INCOMING BLOW

Center pivot point with hand arcing around.

and energy and gets it there just as effectively.

Now within the area of pivot points, there's the very important aspect of blocks. You want to block attacks on or near the pivot point. When you lock your arm and take a blow against the pivot point, the shock is transferred into your arm, which does a shock absorber number. What you don't want to do is block with the tip if you can help it. The reason for this is the tip of your opponent's stick has enough energy to act against you in a negative way. In other words, the force of the blow may make your weapon spin out of your hand by creating a pivot point in the middle of your weapon, whether it was there a minute ago or not.

I could ramble on, but the best way for you to understand the physics of stick fighting is to go out and practice. Now that you know what to look for, you'll be able to catch on more quickly. All of this boils down to body knowledge—things you know so well that when you pick up a stick you know what it's going to take to defend yourself with it. The only way you're going to get that is through practice and experimentation. Pick things up, swing 'em around, bounce 'em off different surfaces, and all that. (Do it all beforehand, or you're going to learn the hard way why knowing this is important.)

Blocks

In fencing, there is a drill called "around the world." It is a sabre technique, and it teaches you the basic blocks you should know. I'm going to bastardize it and make some additions that I have found necessary. There's a count that goes with it, which I have totally forgotten, because as with kata, I'm leery about anything that teaches you to move in a predictable pattern. (That's just me though; I'm paranoid.)

Once again, we break the defense areas into sections. Once again, I vote for ten (with occasional options), and again, others are going to vote for all sorts of different numbers. Use whatever works for you! The goal here is to get the job done, not to be persnickity about technique.

Starting with the assumption that the guy is facing you, we have the body blocks of upper left, upper right, upper upper (yo' head), lower left, lower right, lower lower (yo' nuts), and the four front sections (as described in the quarterstaff chapter).

The side body blocks are done with the stick pointing up or down. They are done in front of the body, but closer than parries, and they will stop most blows to the body. They are easy to learn and

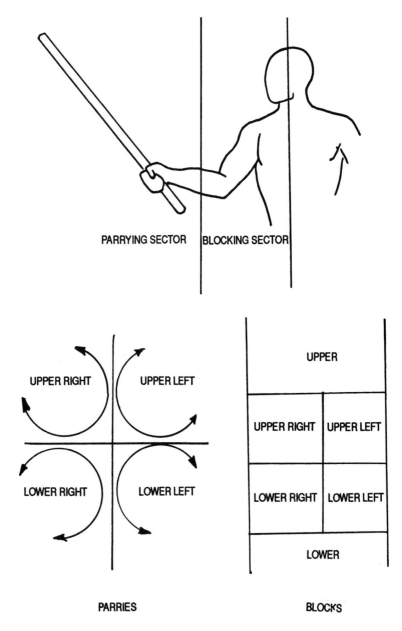

PARRYING SECTOR | BLOCKING SECTOR

UPPER RIGHT   UPPER LEFT

LOWER RIGHT   LOWER LEFT

PARRIES

UPPER

UPPER RIGHT | UPPER LEFT

LOWER RIGHT | LOWER LEFT

LOWER

BLOCKS

Rehash of ten basic fencing sectors.

should be practiced while remembering the boring-ass physics that I just nearly put you to sleep with, especially the one about taking the impact into the V of your hand.

You will note that somewhere along the line the tip of the stick will have to cross the belly button equator. Fear not, you won't have to get married to Neptune's daughter. (Sorry, Navy reference.) What

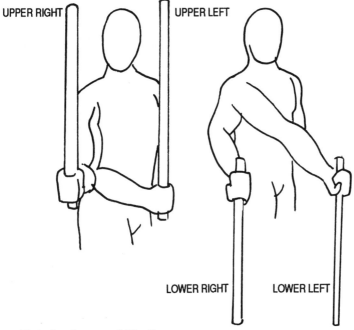

UPPER RIGHT   UPPER LEFT

LOWER RIGHT   LOWER LEFT

Four basic sword blocks.

will happen is somewhere, somehow you will have to pivot your stick. (That's why I bored you about pivot points.) If fencing has one major weakness, this is it. From the "on guard" position (or any other funny shape you find yourself in) it is a bit clumsy to get to lower left guard. This is because you not only have to spin your wrist, you must twist your elbow too. To get to lower right guard, you just have to spin your elbow. (Pick up a stick and you'll see what I'm blabbering about.)

The best and fastest way to do this is to drop your point in front of you rather than to your side. This is because you don't have to move your arm as much when you do it in front of you and you're less likely to do that stupid trick of knocking your opponent's weapon into yourself.

Upper and Lower Guards

In the upper upper section you have two ways to block: left or right. Most formal fencers frown on the

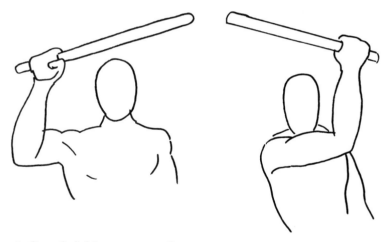

Left and right upper guard.

left side block, thinking it's a rather low form of block, lacking grace. (And in fact it is. But when it comes to a choice of grace or keeping from getting your head split open, grace can bend over and spread 'em.) It's a rather clumsy block from which to get anywhere else defensively. So if you're on the defensive and you find yourself in this position, either backpedal (and buy time) or counterstrike immediately. Its one real strong suit is it's primed for a serious counterstrike against your opponent's weaker side. You can come in with a real basher if you combine whip with arm strength. If the guy sees you swinging in, he's going to have to reconsider leaving it out in the wind, 'cause you're going to knock it off if he don't start defending.

Believe it or not most people are not terribly experienced at guarding their right side. That's why fighting a south paw is such a bitch. The heavy blows are coming from a side you're not accustomed to. When two right-handed guys square off they usually end up thumping on each other's left sides. Their lefts are stronger at blocking, while their rights are stronger at hitting. This is why experienced fighters trade off the hand they lead with.

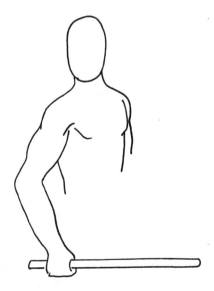

Low block.

The lower guard is another one of those that fencers sneer at. Then again, ball shots are a no-no on the strip. The restrictions are a little bit different on the street. (The Chinese forms have no such problems; they cover the old yangeroo.) This is sort of a stop thrust for gut rippers that come in as a low upward arc.

Front Guards

In the four front sectors, there are two schools of thought—parry or block. Both work within their space. Depending on the situation, one works better than the other. It's up to you figure out which is the so-called "right one."

The parries are the same circular-type movements that were discussed in the quarterstaff chapter. They work best on thrust attacks but can be modified to work on strikes. The reason they work on strikes is that they spin your opponent's weapon out of effective range, leaving him open to counterattack. It takes a little practice to get to this point though.

The bad news is that the same thing can be done against you. There are various things you can do, and they all depend on the exact circumstances in which the pivot occurs. In other words, the only way to learn it is to go out and practice.

Working with blocks in the four front sections, you kind of run into a situational call. These blocks are basically strikes, but instead of striking against your opponent's body, you strike his weapon. This is a real common kendo trick, especially in the lower sections. These blocks are especially effective against strikes. They can work against thrusts, but you had better have your timing down or you're fucked.

That's the problem of using blocks against thrusts. They may not get there in time. In the case of thrusts, "in time" means to deflect the forward

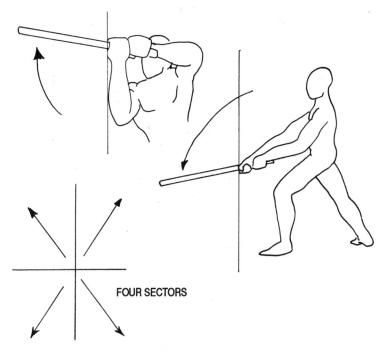

FOUR SECTORS

Front and side view of strike blocks and four sectors.

moving blade into an area of safety before the moment of impact. A parry gets into the center of a blade with a little pressure and causes the end to deflect in a major way. A block against a thrust is dealing with a fast moving end and trying to move it the actual distance necessary for safety. Now, all of this is the theory, and that's why it's theoretically not a good idea to try it. In a practical sense though, sometimes you have to do something that ain't that effective in the long run to keep from getting your

ass poked in the short run. Practice with it, don't
rely only on it, do it, and only when absolutely necessary, and you should be fine.

The Chinese and Filipino styles have all sorts
of other blocks for this, that, and the other thing.
In fact, if you're ever surrounded by ten sword-
wielding samurai, there are all sorts of neat tricks
you can use to defend your back, sides, feet, and
so on. I won't go into these except to say they
exist and you should have at least a passing
knowledge of them. I've seen Chinese sword technique in kata form, but I've never had a chance to
go up against anyone who is really good at it.

At first, you should go out and spend most of
your time practicing blocking and parrying. The
fact that you can cover your ass is more important than the fact that you have a fast strike,
especially if the opponent beats you off the starting line. It is a plain and simple fact of life that
you won't always get to move first. The best way
to deal with this is to be real strong in the defense
department.

Stances

Let's look at stances here for a minute.
Remember I told you about the Japanese samurai
and their little switch-hit suicide game? There's an
interesting side effect. They have a whole lot of
stances that don't cover their asses too well, but
they'll knock the shit out of you if you get too close
to them. These stances can strike with some ugly-
ass efficiency. If you see someone drop into one of
these, either grab a polearm and flatten his point,
throw something at him, or run away. It's time for
the "Fuck this shit, click, BLAM!" attitude, because

unless you're really good, the guy is going to take you with him.

This has a lot to do with why people think kendo is so good. It has a personal disdain for injury that borders on the psychotic (something like a drunk marine). If your goal is purely to attack, kendo's where it's at, but there's more to survival than just attacking. It's a bitch to deal with, yes, but then again so were the kamikaze, and look how many of them are still hanging around.

The absolute worst kendo stance to have to deal with is the overhead grip, known among smartasses

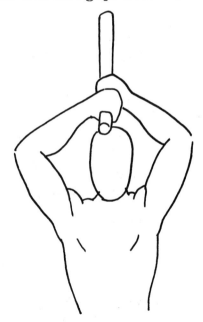

Lightning rod stance.

like me as the "lightning rod stance." (I keep on wishing a bolt of lightning would fry the son of a bitch who strikes this pose and save me all sorts of trouble.) It's a great position from which to clobber anybody getting anywhere near you. Its one weakness is thrown cue balls . . . oh, and small furniture, bullets, frisbeed ashtrays, and anything resembling a polearm. Those and slashing hacks at the head and arms will usually interrupt the guy's concentration.

The baseball (or "Babe Ruth") stance is another bitch to deal with for the simple reason of the power it has. There's a proper name for it, but I can't find it in my library anywhere. If you walk into this,

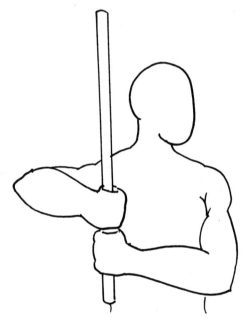

Babe Ruth stance (Chinese).

either be wearing full armor or come in blocking. Strikes can come in from overhand and underhand, so watch your ass when dealing with it or you'll get knocked into last week. It does have a serious weakness though—the entire left side. So if you can slip his guard, attack that side.

I think this one is called the "sleeping sword," or

if you've encountered it, the "nut knocker." The
sleeping sword can wake up on you real fuckin' fast.
It looks so stupid that you think you can just walk

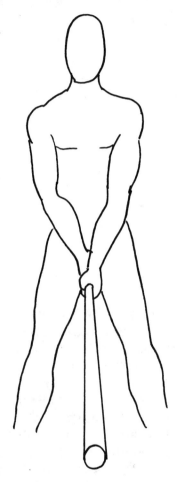

Sleeping sword.

over and bean the guy on the head. It isn't and you
can't. A kendo snap from this point will either put
your breeding days to an end or turn your knees to
jellified mush. Fortunately a rolled trash can will

also wake up the sleeping sword and save your nuts at the same time.

Here's one from those guys I told you about earlier, the Society for Creative Anachronisms (SCA). It looks real dorky until you get close to it, then you're going to get your ass blasted over the state line.

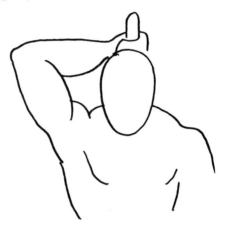

SCA stance.

Thing about it is, you don't know *which* state line it's gonna be. This is a major flexible stance—the guy can cream you from left, right, overhead or any other direction he chooses. If he squats or straightens his legs, you don't know which level he's going to hit you at either. Go out and play with this one and you'll see just how dangerous it is.

These stances are all real tempting to go waddling into. Most people don't think about it from the standpoint of "Why's the guy leaving that flapping out in the wind like that?" Instead they think the guy has just done a major code stupid and just walk in, thereby committing one themselves. If you're up against somebody who does something weird like one of these stances, seriously consider

running away. Even if you've gone out and practiced all sorts of stuff, if you haven't encountered it
before on the practice mat, don't push it in the

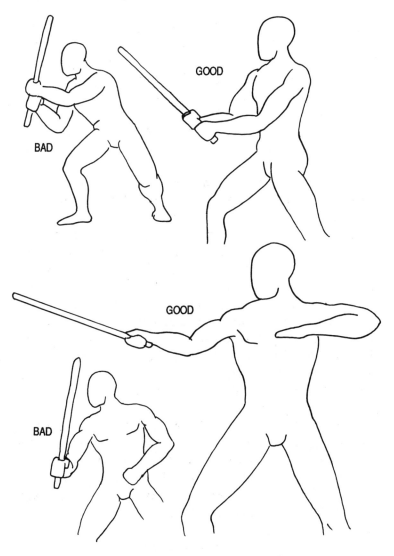

Good and bad kendo (top) and fencing (bottom) stances.

streets. There are no sensei to stop the pounding if something goes wrong out there.

The ready positions of fencing and kendo are a little more well known. They also are more flexible for protecting yourself or attacking. When most people grab something, they will drop into a parody of these stances. You will have to know by simple sight who's trained and who isn't by the way they grab something. Once you know about balance, mobility, guard, and other stuff relating to fighting, you'll know how to spot who's trained and who isn't. Look at the photos on the previous page and guess who is and isn't trained.

One of the real cocksuckers you'll encounter are those styles that look relaxed. The guy will be standing there with the stick held loosely in his hand, point down, no real stance, just feet shoulder width apart, body slightly turned, guard down, and totally relaxed. LOOK OUT! The guy has speed, mobility, striking strength, and a strong guard going for him. Usually the guys who are really good take this stance. It's something most punks don't know about and they had better not cross it or they will discover a whole new meaning of pain. Remember what I said about being able to keep cool when you know you're covered? Watch for people who are too calm for the situation.

Another thing to watch for is styles that use two sticks. If the person knows what he is doing, it's like dealing with a coked-out windmill. He'll be all over you from every which way. Fortunately, most of these styles rely on shorter sticks and can be dealt with by keeping your distance.

I've mostly shot my wad about stick fighting. Now it's up to you to go out and practice. One thing you can do to start practicing is to get a stick that fits your hand comfortably and start twirling it around. Grab it by the end and spin it down and back up again on both sides. Careful or you'll bash yourself (on your left side if you're right handed, on your right side if you're left-handed). To do this, you'll have to relax your wrist. Here's where it gets tricky. When the stick is pointed upward, stop it. You want to be able to stop the stick without wiggling the tip. The goal is to get to the point where when you stop the stick, it's like it just ran into a wall of wet clay. No bounce, shake, or vibrations, just a dead stop. I would advise doing this outside at first until you get an idea of what the extended reach is. I have a roommate who put several sword holes in our living room ceiling before he learned how much this kind of stuff extended his reach.

Your best bet is to go out and grab some form of schooling, whether it be fencing, martial arts, or the SCA. This will teach you to react instinctively to what's going on around you. As you wander around, practice looking at things from the standpoint of how you would use them as a weapon. At first you may get confused, but try to keep what I've said here in mind. After awhile it'll all become obvious to you.

Strike Enhancers

Most people are not really aware of the endless variety of strike enhancers. My jaw still clicks sometimes to commemorate my own graduation from ignorance.

If it's small, hard, and makes your strikes more damaging, it's a strike enhancer. If it makes your strikes harder, it's an impact weapon. If it does more damage than your bare hands alone, it's a ripper. Sometimes it's both.

The major impact weapons are yawara sticks, saps, brass knuckles, and punch gloves. Punch rings, tiger claws, and spiked gauntlets fall into the ripper category. Let's look at how these types of weapons can affect you.

Impact Weapons

A yawara stick is a hand-held hunk of hard wood or iron that increases the hardness of the hand when striking. That's like the official designation. What I'm going to be referring to as a yawara stick is anything you can grab—a hairbrush, roll of

coins, lipstick container, lighter, socket wrench, pipe
fitting, or steel dowel—to make your blow hit harder.
It's whatever is around to help you knock the guy's
teeth down his throat a little easier.

A sap is a blackjack-like item. It's not as big as a
billy (or short club). Cops still like to carry them
because they can hit someone with it and it just
looks like they nailed the guy with their hand.
Nobody saw a billy club. This is why they are illegal
in California and a few other states. People don't see
them. They can be flexible or inflexible depending
on the degree of improvisation.

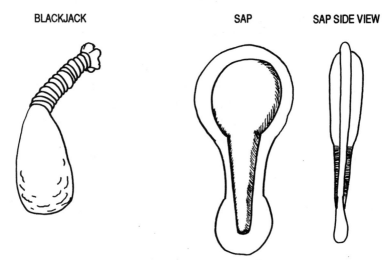

BLACKJACK   SAP   SAP SIDE VIEW

A sap is a blackjack-like item.

Strictly speaking, a sap can be anything from a
bar of soap in a sock to a real blackjack to a shoe
(don't laugh, I've been beaned with and bonked others with shoes and they hurt like hell) to a socket
wrench or, my favorite embarrassing one, a pot.

Brass knuckles are a bitch. I've only been

attacked by real ones once. The guy started to swing and something warned me not to block but to dodge. When I did, I saw something flash by my face. I backpedaled and did my monkey-in-a-zoo imitation—I started throwing shit at him. By the time he shrugged a couple of beer bottles off his chest, three guys fell on him. End of that one. I don't know if brass knuckles are legal anywhere in America, but you can wrap chains around your hand or use an oyster shelling knife as a damn good equivalent. A serious set of rings doubles as the same thing.

One way we used to get busted for fighting in school was that our knuckles would be fucked up after fights. You punch the guy in the mouth and you cut your hand on his teeth. Red, bruised, bloody knuckles really undermined our attempts at denying we had been fighting. (Of course brawling in the classroom kind of fucked up my alibi, too.) What we needed was some way to protect the hands from visible abuse, yet not reduce the impact by padding. The answer was the ominous black leather punch glove (see, isn't Michael Jackson just soooo tough?). We were smart, but it turned out others had faced this dilemma before us, starting with the Roman gladiators. You can have the simple light leather gloves to protect your knuckles or you can have gloves with lead strips across the knuckles and yawara sticks sewn into the palms or some of the outrageous punk-rock spiked gloves (which, by the way, if cheaply made are only good for one, maybe two blows).

Rippers

In the ripper category, you have all sorts of nasty shit. They aren't too pleasant by themselves, but combined with weight, they get into seriously ugly. An old roomie of mine had a set of brass knuckles that had the equivalent of punch-ring rippers on each of the knuckles. (Blech!)

If you want to see the best collection of punch rings around, walk into a biker bar. If you want to see how much damage they can do to a human face, pick a fight. The two favorite symbols of bikerdom are the eagle (Harley, America, and freedom) and the Vikings (drunken looting and pillaging). In case you haven't noticed, eagles have claws and beaks, and Vikings have horned helmets and forked beards.

Eagle punch rings. Claws and beaks make good rippers.

Stylized into jewelry these make some big pieces with sharp points all over them. Not only does the guy look, smell, and act like a grizzly bear on acid, he's got claws on his paws. If the impact doesn't get you, the loss of blood will.

Tiger claws are from India. (It's funny how

many people don't think of those little guys fighting. They can and do. The British were always sending troops to India to keep those crazy bastards from kicking the Empire out on its snobby ass.) Anyway, tiger claws are officially called *bagh nakh*. These are sort of related to the ninja claws, but they're less for rock climbing and sword catching. What they are is four (sometimes five) blades connected to a metal strip. This strip is held in the palm of your hand while the claws stick out between your fingers.

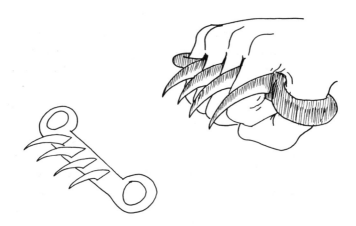

Tiger claws, officially referred to as *bagh nakh*.

The story behind them is they were the weapon of assassins and thieves, who would tear people up with them. Since the claw effect resembled that of a tiger attack, the assault could be passed off as Tony coming out of the hills hungry for something other than cereal.

A set of keys held in the hand this way is a relative of *bagh nakh* (doesn't that sound like somebody with a chest cold?).

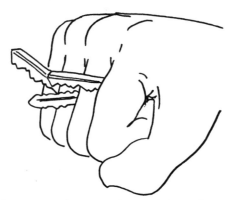

A set of keys can be transformed into improvised *bagh nakh*.

Small blades are often held this way; razors, pen knives, nails, drywall screws, pieces of scrap metal, and, in dire emergencies, even toothpicks can be used in this regard.

Gauntlets can be anything from an annoyed porcupine to armor. The heavy metal, leather-and-stud, rock-and-roll crowd is real fond of these things. If used right, they are a mother to go up against. They either turn the arm into a mace on the attack or a spike wall on the defense. Less exotic ones can be found floating around various industries in the form of heavy work gloves. Officially, a gauntlet (unless modified) is more for defense than offense. Since we are talking about using improvised items for self-defense, this weapon applies. Ever picked up a welder's glove? Think that would be safe to grab a knife blade with? Think about it. Now, on with how to use these things.

Fighting with Strike Enhancers

Yawara sticks, I believe, are Okinawan, although they could be Japanese. If you know how to throw a

punch, you know how to use these. There are, however, variations. Make a fist around a roll of dimes
and look at your hand. How many hitting surfaces
do you have? The minimum answer should be five.
Look at the illustration below.

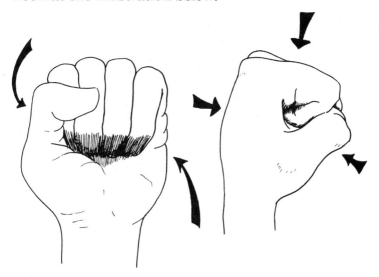

Fist with striking surfaces.

What makes a yawara stick a bitch to deal with
is that you can strike from any angle. A swing back,
hook, upper thrust, straight punch, or backhand
are all enhanced by yawara sticks. Their major
shortcoming is that your punch has to land in order
to make them work. That means if you go up
against somebody who knows how to fight in general, and against these in particular, you might be in
trouble. The way to fight against somebody who has
a yawara in their hands is to dodge a lot and slap
block.[3] Another trick is to block and strike against

[3] Explained in detail in *Cheap Shots, Ambushes and Other
Lessons.*

your opponent's wrists, thereby transmitting the damage to his arms, slowing him down, and potentially causing him to drop it. Come to think of it, backpedal and hit him with a chair—it's easier.

If you are up against a better fighter and you have something you're using as a yawara stick, go for his arms, especially the upper arms. After you do damage there, move to his thighs. Hopefully, this'll slow him down enough for you to make good on your exit.

I was talking about a yawara stick that fits inside your hand. Often, you'll pick something up that extends out past your hand, like a hairbrush, socket wrench, scissors, or a big stapler. This makes your arm have an L shape to it, which is especially good for trapping and hooking. If somebody throws a blow at you, this can be used to "scoop up" your opponent's limb and lift and spin it to one side. Most people have never been hooked this way before and don't know that it can happen.

In the same situation, strikes are more severe with the yawara stick. While they can be used as short billies by a wrist snap, it's not always effective to do so. What is effective is to "stab" with them (if it's sharp or pointed, there is a good chance it *will* stab the person, so keep that in mind). If it's blunt, it serves as a "spike punch." What this means is that all of the energy of your blow will go into an area of roughly one square inch. While the energy would be the same if you were to hit someone with your fist, it would be distributed over a much wider area. With the yawara stick, the energy is more concentrated, and therefore more damaging. Be careful of these blows to the head. The spike punch can literally punch a hole in someone's head. If they die, it could mean a murder rap for you.

Saps are either flexible or inflexible. They utilize mostly a wrist snap/whip technique. Leather saps are still sold in police supply stores, so don't tell me they don't still carry them. Most people think a sap is used to knock people out. True, but if it hits *anywhere* it's going to do damage. Swing a sap at somebody's leg and that leg is going to be out of action for a while. It's hard to run away doing a combo of the mummy walk and a pogo hop. Beer bottles make great sap-like devices, as do shoes. Ever been slapped by a tennis shoe, much less a hard leather shoe? It'll make your eyes water. (The hardness of the sap you're attacking with will determine whether it's just an opening shot or the end of the conversation. A beer bottle will usually put them down, but a tennis shoe will just stun them. It's up to you to use that stunned time to land a few heavier gifts upside his head.)

One of the weaknesses of saps (especially if they're flexible) is that they are pretty much limited to the offense. This means that if the person mounts a counteroffensive, you could be in some shit. Most of the strikes will be a combo of arm swing and whip/snap. Because of this, the sap can leave a hole in your defenses if you're not careful. A lot of people want to pull way the fuck back to strike; actually, you don't have to. If you don't want to leave yourself open, you'll need to practice striking in tight areas. This is mostly done with tight wrist work and the arm muscle tightening at the moment of impact.

In my old neighborhood, older women were fond of carrying a sock with a bar of soap in it. It was a great combo of sap and flail that could be disassembled into totally legal parts if the cops showed up. It wasn't as likely to be fatal, but it would knock the shit out of any young punk who messed with them.

Punch rings are something that deserve a moment's notice. There are two ways to use these—slow and powerful or fast and messy. Let's take what most people consider a biker to be—big, fuzzy, greasy, tough, and mean. Well, except that bikers vary in size, that's pretty much right. (I should point out that cowboys wear these, too. Bikers and cowboys have a whole lot more in common than they like to admit. They use each other's taste in clothing as an excuse not to talk to each other.) Let's look at the big fuzzies. Sometimes you'll see these guys wearing two meat-grinder rings on each finger. There's a good reason for this: it diffuses the impact against their fingers, meaning they're less likely to break their fingers when they knock you through a wall. This also explains the huge honker punch rings that run from knuckle to knuckle. These also distribute the impact to prevent broken fingers.

Those are the ones that hit hard. There are also rings that hit fast. These are usually smaller and just as sharp. If you have a small ring you have to hit fast and repeatedly. If you try to hit too hard, you run a very good chance of breaking your finger. Another thing you can do is to wrap and pad your ring to act as a shock absorber.

Tiger claws and related stuff have similar problems. If they are held loosely they can twist and cut your fingers. Since you also have swipes to contend with, you have to be careful. Another bitch to deal with is the damage to the inside of your hand. Let's look at brass knuckles for a minute, too. The absolute best sort of brass knuckles you can get have a weird cleat-shaped part that rests in your palm.

GOOD CONSTRUCTION

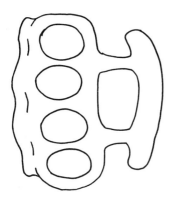

BAD CONSTRUCTION

Good brass knuckles like the set at left have an extra cleat that rests in the palm.

This transfers the impact of the striking part into the palm, and from there, into the wrist and arm. This keeps the damage down on your end.

What you really have to know is that impact force goes both ways. These things allow you to hit hard, but unless you take precautions, you're going to get hurt. Look at it this way. If you wrap a chain around your knuckle and punch somebody, the chain serves to concentrate that impact. That means it's going to hurt the other guy more. However, forty years ago this little guy came up with a theory that says "E=mc²," or in simple terms, "For every action there is an equal and opposite reaction." *That means an equal amount of concentrated energy is coming back into your hand!* Your bones are just as susceptible to breaking as the guy you're hitting, especially since the energy coming back is just as concentrated as what you're dishing out. So, yes, you're mauling his face, but at the same time you're mauling your hand.

This is why good brass knuckles have that extra cleat—it acts as a transference system. Gloves protect your hands by padding some of the impact. (The best punch rings are triangular. In the front they're pointed, but in the back they're broad-based. The best are also designed to cover the finger from knuckle to knuckle, acting as a shock distributor over the entire finger.) Properly designed tiger claws are locked down into place by the hand so they don't twist.

If you use improvised tiger-claw systems, know that they will twist on you. Not only is the other guy going to get fucked up, so is your hand. Keys, nails, and screws will twist and tear your hand up. If you punch with them, they are driven into your palm. Blades held in this position twist and slice nerves, tendons, and blood vessels, all of which can seriously reduce your hand movement. Don't think it can't happen to you. I have a stiff index finger with limited mobility from a cut I once took across the knuckle. If you have a choice of weapons in an improvised situation, you should seriously consider grabbing something else. Yawara sticks are more flexible and easier on the hands.

Gauntlets are your friends. I love gauntlets; they allow you to do all sorts of shit that you normally can't do safely. Depending on their construction, they can be an offensive aid, a defensive aid, or both. The offensive kind are the ones the heavy-metal head-bangers and punkers like. These are usually black leather with all sorts of studs, spikes, rivets, and conchos all over them. When you take away all the leather and mousse, these people are usually skinny, unhealthy kids, but you do have to look out for these things. When used right, a heavy, studded wrist band is a mace with concentrated impact points that'll send you into la-la land right quick.

The spikes are a bitch to deal with, because even though they break off easily, they still leave sharp points that you have to deal with. (By the way, if you buy one of these things, look at the back. What you don't want to see is the back of the spikes. If it isn't leather lined, line it. If you hit somebody without a lining, these things will come loose and tear up your hand.) If you're not a trained fighter, going up against a spiked opponent is not a good idea. Step back and start throwing things or pick up a distance weapon—it's easier than trying to mess with them. Somebody who wears spikes has to contend with the fact that people may not want to play in his range.

The studded wristbands are less offensively inclined. This does not mean they can't be used as such, it's just that people are less likely to think about using them as such. Lock your wrist (or arm) and use either your elbow or shoulder as a pivot point and you have a mace. The Chinese fighting forms (especially the crane) deal with striking with the wrist. If you know how to do it, it really widens your striking capabilities. For example, if you're standing next to me, I can still knock you on your ass without turning towards you. Most of the moves I know include wrist strikes and back-of-the-hand techniques. If you're interested in keeping your nose glued on, I'd suggest going and checking into these things.

On the defense is where gauntlets pay their way. It may look tougher on your right, but the best place to wear armor is where it is needed. This is why you should wear it on your left side. The odds are against you fighting a southpaw. This means that most incoming blows are going to be coming in from your left side. The armor afforded by a gauntlet can be priceless. I used to wear a leather wristband on my left hand; it took everything from bludgeon hits to knife slashes to straight-out punches. To this day, my attitude is, "My hide or cowhide, guess which one I'd rather leave on the pavement?" Plain leather works well by itself. It's less obvious—and therefore less threatening—to people around you.

If, however, you're really into being a stud, studded is where it's at. The studded version is great for stopping slashes from razors, broken bottles, and knives. Also, the studded are better suited to stopping puncturing, ripping impact weapon combos like rakes, shovels, hayhooks and improvised maces (a 2 x 4 with nails, for instance). The bad news is you have to exchange extra protection for conspicuousness. If somebody sees all of those flashy studs and points, he's not going to try and come in through your strongest section, he's going to be paying attention to how to hit you in your weak spots. All your guard must reflect this added strength to one section.

Another thing about studded wristbands is they cause damage when they are used to block. If somebody throws a punch at you and you block his blow, your impact with the studs and points is going to be harder than with just your arm.

I nearly fell out of my chair laughing when I saw it, because it was the perfect combo of protection and camouflage. It was a New York fashion—studded jackets. I saw one with the arms thickly studded around the wrists and tapered off up the arm. Talk about the perfect cover for a gauntlet! It's armor disguised as style. You can wear this into a place looking flashy and not scare people, and you can walk through bad areas knowing that you're protected against most kinds of weapons. If you really wanted to get ultraprotected, sew heavy leather into the forearms. Do the same with your regular jacket if you feel that wearing studs wouldn't fit your image. That way you can move around being inconspicuous about being armored.

Work gloves are truly charming for the protection they afford, both as padding against impact and protection against cuts. My preferred fighting style against almost any form is with a weapon in my right hand and a gauntleted left hand. In this capacity, I am pure hell. I've gone against knives and clubs in real fights this way, and in practice I've gone against swords, spears, flails, bills, and a whole host of other things. The protection afforded by gloves is incredible. It doesn't make you God, but it surely adds to your self-defense technique.

In an emergency, like against somebody who pulls an edged weapon, you should employ improvised gauntlets if possible. Grab a shirt, jacket, or a towel and wrap it around your left arm. This will afford some necessary protection.

One thing you can do is take a plain leather gauntlet and wear it under long sleeves. Since the thing's got to be cut back for wrist movement anyway, the cuff of the sleeve will keep it mostly covered. By the way, find out how far your sleeve slides back by extending your arm out from your body, then put the gauntlet about one inch back from there. This is if you're in places where they really get weirded out about the reality of violence (like if you're a driver for an office that sends you out into some shady neighborhoods).

Another way to do these without looking like you're up to anything other than odd taste in clothes is watchbands. If you go to swap meets or

Mexico, you can still find those 1970s Hercules wristwatch bands. They do exactly what I was talking about, but at the cost of a watch. (Better it take the lickin'.) In the same territory, although they're not as hard as leather, are what are called "commando" watchbands. These are canvas and velcro thingamabobs, with a flap that covers the watch proper. This is so nobody sees the glow of your watch numbers and shoots you for being where you're not supposed to be.

Let's say you're really into ass kicking and you don't care if you scare the taxpayers. I mean you walk down the street and the testosterone proceeds you by twenty yards, women swoon, and men feel faint of heart. I got a goody for you. Not only do you take a studded and spiked leather gauntlet (seriously, alternate the spikes with those big square pointed studs—it's both for protection and attack that way), but you run off to a restaurant supply store and get something called a butcher's glove. Some cutlery stores carry them, too. The old style is made out of fine mesh chain mail, while the new ones are made out of Kevlar. These gloves are immune to knife cuts, sort of like a king snake is immune to a rattlesnake. For the most part it's effective, but there are limits. This glove can take a few strikes, but don't sit there and saw on it. Anyway, attach this to your gauntlet and you have what is called a knife-fighting gauntlet. These are worn by the real serious hard asses on special occasions. Like when somebody is after them. The bad part about this is people in the know will look at you and decide it might be easier just to shoot you.

I advise wearing gauntlets if you're going into an area where fighting is common, like the street, rowdy honkey tonks, and such. They don't replace common sense, but they do slow down the incoming abuse level (and this is what it's all about—not looking like you just stepped out of a Steve Reeves movie).

Flexible Weapons

If you don't know what you're doing, flexible weapons are for first strike only. You had better hope you hit the guy on the first shot, because if he gets off a counterattack, you're screwed. You might be able to keep attacking in hopes of keeping him off balance so he isn't able to muster a counterattack, but I wouldn't count on that happening.

I was in a bullwhip fight once. You know what? That's three times too many. Fighting a flexible weapon is an ugly experience because there really isn't a defense against it except "don't get hit." This can be accomplished with a shield or by just not being there. Flexible weapon against flexible weapon is a bitch for both sides because it's basically go until one side drops from damage or backs off.

Flexible weapons come in three basic types: impact, ripper/cutters, and trappers. They also come in the three different ranges: close, distance, and projectile (in this case, thrown). Examples of these are a bar of soap in a sock (blackjack, close range), nunchucks (actually both close and distance), whips, chains, garrotes

115

(strangling cords), bolos (flying traps), lassos, gusaris (chains with weights), and flails. (Flails are not maces; a mace is a club with a weight on the end. They're fixed weapons. However a stick with a ball and chain is called a flail. In that sense, nunchucks are flails too.)

It doesn't take a lot of brains to figure out what the most common attack with these sort of things is. You pick it up and swing at the guy. If you hit him, great; if not, try again. This goes on until he either gets hit, runs away, or retaliates. If he retaliates, you're in trouble.

This is what's wrong with the way most people use flexible weapons, which is almost always offensively. *This is not a movie!* People counterattack! If you don't know how to defend with flexible weapons, you're going to cash it in real quick.

The easiest way to defend is in the same way you use a quarterstaff. Grab hold of both ends and practice blocking with it. You know the blocks as well as I do by now, so I'm not going to bother repeating myself.

There are two ways to use these blocks: one is hard and the other is soft. Let's use a chain as an example. If you grab the chain on both ends and pull it tight, this is hard. You can use this to block a swing or a strike. It'll impact and bounce off. In this sense, it's like a quarterstaff. The soft style is a trapping style. While the grip is as tight, the tension is looser than the hard style. That's because when the blow is struck the blow will impact is absorbed into the chain like a pillow. When the movement is arrested, you wrap the chain around your opponent's weapon.

Practice swinging and catching chains, ropes, and such until you get to the point where you can

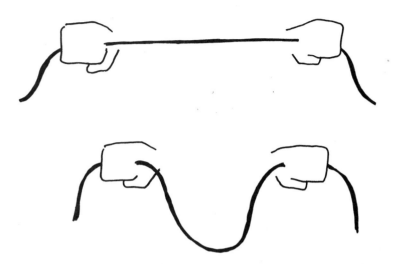

Tight and loose chain guards.

get it back into guard from any position. Switch
hands and practice with both. Practice whip snaps
at different distances with different items. Different
types of chain handle differently, and all handle differently than rope.

The Filipinos and the Chinese have the best for-
malized flexible weapons techniques. In wu shu (a
Chinese gung fu technique), they have chain whips
that have knives on the end. The Filipinos have
pananandata. A common Filipino weapon is called
"monkey balls." This is a rope with ball knots on
both ends, and it can knock the shit out of you big
time if you get hit by it. Next in line are the
Japanese flexible weapon forms. Okinawan forms
are good for flexibles; ninjutsu also has some real
creative ways to whack you one.

I know a guy who used to break up gang fights
with a ten-foot bullwhip. It only takes getting hit
once by one of those to know why you should get
the fuck out of its way. If you're ever faced with a

well-handled whip, you should start throwing rocks. Big rocks, hard rocks, and, if possible, sharp ones.

The so-called "crack of the whip" is actually the sound barrier being broken. A small sonic boom occurs. That means the tip of the mother is going about eight hundred miles per hour. If it hits you anywhere, it's going to do serious damage. If the guy's good, he's going to take out your eye or shave off an ear. I'm serious about how accurate someone can get. I can take a rock off a fence post without hitting the post. We used to practice by targeting certain leaves on branches and taking them off, and I'm not that good. I've heard of stories about the teamsters of the Old West being able to take a fly off an ear of one of their team horses.

The thing about whips is that they are weapons best used in open space. These are something you want to use to keep people away from you. If someone manages to get past the outer guard, you can reverse your grip and use the butt as a gusari. The butt of a bullwhip can thunk somebody pretty hard.

Chains move differently than rope. Some chain is actually twisted to make it look prettier. This type of chain actually twists and binds easier than plain link chain, which is why it's not so hot in the middle of nunchucks. If you carry this kind of chain, it *can* happen.

Light rope can be used as a whip better than chain. Heavy rope can impact someone seriously if used right. It's also real painful to be on the wrong end of a rubber hose.

Bolos are something that can really convince a running person that they want to talk with the ants. A length of thrown chain will wrap somebody's legs up pretty good. Monkey balls are good for this, too. See what's around that you might be able to use in this regard. A weight on the end of a chain can knock somebody pretty good if it's wrapped around the head.

Garrotes are a nasty thing. There are two types: chokers and cutters. Any rope, chain, necktie, belt, or even shoelace can be used as a choker. The more unpleasant kinds have handles and are made out of wire. These mothers can decapitate people. The way to use one is to hold it in both hands; about twenty-four inches is what I like. Practice on a fence post or something inanimate. (I've seen a guy try to do it on somebody without knowing how to do it right. He got stomped.) With both hands behind your target, begin to snake one around the post in a circle. Pass one hand over the other. When this happens, your garrote will be in a tightening noose around the post. If you are even thinking about using this weapon, you have to be fast and strong. The way to foil one of these is to slam your chin into your chest.

Gusaris and flails are a real sons of bitches to deal with because they are a blend of whip (speed and mobility) and mace (crushee you headee).

Gusaris are not things you want to be anywhere near.

These are not things that you want to be anywhere near. If someone pulls out something like this and begins to look like he knows what he's doing, start throwing furniture. If there's a trash can lid around, it's time to take up shield fighting (something the SCA does a lot of).

Diversions

This is a different sort of chapter because it deals primarily with first moves to shock your opponent long enough to clobber him. The number of moves that exist is almost endless. I have always followed the beer supply. Where it goes, I go, so it should come as no surprise to anybody the number of times I have opened fights by throwing my beer at somebody and landing hard on him a second later.

I have a friend who was confronted by two guys in a bathroom while he was taking a leak. He turned and pissed on them. While they were standing there in shock, he blasted past them. It's incredible the number of stories my friends and I have on this subject. We can sit around for hours telling them until we have to stop because our sides hurt from laughing so much. The area of diversions is really where most improvised weapons are used, and it's what you have to watch out for, because if you don't, you're going to end up in a world of shit. If it looks like you're going to get into a fight, there are a couple of things you can do to reduce your chances of getting nailed.

Step one. *If the guy doesn't have anything in his hands and he makes a move to pick something up, CALL HIM ON IT!* Tell him to freeze right there and get his hand away from it. If he keeps moving, hit him. Hit him hard and hit him fast! Keep on hitting him until he's down. (If the guy keeps going for it after you've called him on it, you can be 99 percent sure he's going to hit you with it.)

Step two. *If the guy has something in his hand, get something in your hand.* If he mentions it, tell him you're just evening the odds. It's best if you can say it with an easy smile and a drawl. That's an "oh shit" sign if ever there was one. People who smile about fighting are not people you want to tangle with.

Step three. *Never let his hands out of your sight!* Honest to God, you never know what's going to show up in them if you do. I almost died learning this one, so listen up good here.

Step four. *Scope out what's around his hand.* If there's anything that can be used, tell him to get his hand away from it—*now.* If he gives you any shit about it, bean the motherfucker before he gets you.

Step five. *In the beginning, it's okay to look in the guy's eyes, but if it looks like it's going to go down no matter what you say, don't look at the eyes of somebody you're going to mix it up with; look at his shoulders.* There's a thing you should know about called "broadcasting." Most people, whether trained or untrained, will move certain parts of their body in preparation for a strike. Very few can throw a punch without tensing and shifting their shoulders in ways that are easily recognizable. This is especially true of kicks. Unless the guy is in a kicking position already, he's going to have to shift his weight to kick. Watch a martial arts class and see what I mean. In time, you'll learn to watch for these signs in your peripheral vision, but in the meantime it doesn't matter 'cause paying all that attention to what's happening at shoulder level makes it look like you're going to rip the guy's throat out.

Those are the basics. If you want to know more about what to watch for to keep from getting hit, read my first book.[4] The rest of these things consists of knowing what can be used as a diversionary attack; ergo, what is a potential threat.

Liquids are your friends. I personally can't believe the number of people who A) start a fight with someone with a drink in their hand and B) don't realize what a golden opportunity a drink is. If you have it, splash it! My God, soda and citrus juices thrown in your eyes sting like shit! Ever tried to see through a chocolate shake? They aren't very transparent. Those are the nonalcoholic drinks. Think about gin in the eyes. Yeech! (Kinda sums up my feeling for gin anyway. Blecch! If you like it, you can have my share.)

If you are carrying a Coke in a cup with a lid and it looks like you're going to get into it, squeeze the cup and displace the lid. This will allow the liquid to exit faster. Start looking around and seeing how many times you could splash, soak, or dampen people with liquids.

Bars offer a wide variety of offensive diversions. They also have a lot of stuff you can use to throw at people. Salted peanuts, aside from increasing your thirst so you buy more drinks, can have great shotgun effects. Peanuts flying everywhere, and all that

---

[4] Also explained in *Cheap Shots, Ambushes and Other Lessons*. Christ, I feel like a fuckin' professor: "Refer back to my original thesis on the subject of motivations for inebriated aggression."

salt in the eyes. Boy, that's real comfortable. Ashtrays fall along the same lines. The obnoxious stuff in the eyes is painful enough as is, but when you hit him with the bowl it's even worse.

Pick up a half-full trash can and let it fly mouth first. If it hits him, it hurts; it also slimes him in garbage. Frisbeeing a metal trash can lid is also a good way to catch somebody's attention.

Chairs don't fly too much by themselves, but with your help they do. Ever looked at a chair from the standpoint of how to catch a flying one? I'll give you a hint—don't even try. A flying chair is something you really would be happier avoiding altogether. If someone throws one at you and you can't get out of the way, your best bet would be to try and parry it with another chair. (By the way, you can dodge by just collapsing your knees. Ain't no rules say you have to dodge sideways only.)

Spitting in someone's face is also a great way to start a lasting friendship. If you do though, you better start beating on the person with all your might to make sure he goes down and stays down. The shock value from getting spit on is incredible. There was a study a few years back that discovered people react worse to getting spit on than they do to getting hit. I learned about this one personally. The last physical fight my brother and I were in was when I accidently spit on him. I was talking to somebody else as I opened the door to spit. He was coming in the door at the same time. It got ugly.

One thing that never ceases to amaze me is the number of times people will start shit while standing in the most God-awful places. I mean, tell me, was it smart for the guy to try and pick a fight with me at the side of the pool? Another guy while standing with his back to a curb? Or the most spectacular one of my entire career, in front of a beer display in a liquor store? (The owner looked at me and said, "He started it, he pays for it.") The answer to these and many other questions is, "Hell no!" One push, that's all it took. I have also seen a guy pick a fight at the top of stairs (he went to the hospital), on the Venice pier (he went for a swim) and on roller skates (he went down)! I mean, *get real, people.* Look around and see what's in your terrain. A shove to the guy in just the right way could solve your problems real quick. The same can be said for you, so watch where you are standing before you get into it.

Briefcases can be swung up into the family jewels of an annoying person or used as an expensive but effective shield. They are a little cumbersome on the offensive, but you can't have everything.

In regard to throwing things, if you can pick it up, you can throw it. Anybody who has ever played baseball can tell you what it feels like to catch one in the chest. Pool balls hurt more. In general, the harder the object the harder the impact. (Food fights are kind of fun. We had a vice principal in school who was dumb enough to walk into one. My God, Poncho Villa didn't get such a reception as this guy did.)

Pool cues make great impromptu javelins if you can't get there in time. So do brooms, mops, shovels, and anything else long and stick-like.

Throwing cats is something that will piss off the SPCA, but catching a cat will get you stitches in places you didn't know you had. I know a guy who almost blinded his uncle that way, and he was just playing.

For people who learn by osmosis, hardbound books are handy. If you throw them by the spine, they flap apart quickly. This slows them down but turns them into the equivalent of a flying set of keys. (Why *do* people toss you a set of keys? I mean, I don't know about you, but the idea of catching a flying porcupine does not excite me in ways I like to be excited. I can understand pegging somebody with them in a fight, but when friends toss them to ya, you have to wonder about their childhood. Like did they pull wings off of butterflies or something?) You can grab a book a certain way and with a flip get it to fly about five feet before it opens up.

Oh, by the way, have you ever seen somebody snap bottle caps? They put them between their fingers and then snap their fingers. It sends the bottle caps flying. (We used to sit on the roof drinking beer and seeing if we could fire them into the neighbor's backyard. We didn't like our neighbor.) I have met several people who could snap razor blades in the same manner. I never figured out how they did it, so I can't tell you, but I've seen it done.

Playing cards, believe it or not, can be frisbeed pretty hard. In fact, you can actually kill people with them if you get good enough. It's a matter of speed. There used to be a guy whose entire act consisted of throwing cards and doing other card tricks. They clocked him throwing cards upwards of two hundred miles an hour. The guy went big game hunting in Africa and bagged an antelope with a card! He also wrote a book about it years ago that I'm not sure is still in print but could possibly be found in used bookstores. I taped razor blades onto the cards I threw. It's like getting hit with a buzz saw. Once I threw one at a guy that missed him but stuck in a wall near him. He decided it was time to leave; it was getting too serious.

I could ramble on and on about improvised weapons, but I think you have the general idea of what it takes to learn how to use them. With the basics comes the knowledge that you can use damn near anything to defend yourself if you know what general category it falls into. Much of what gets people hurt in this business is that they don't pay attention to the critical points of fighting.

Most of what you learned in this book can be called the critical points. These are the things that go wrong the most or are not taught in formal martial art schools. The fact that this stuff isn't taught isn't necessarily a reflection on the style or the teacher. It's more along the lines of they don't know what it's like out in the real world with scared and unpredictable people. Most people never end up in a place where they need this kind of knowledge. That's okay. Personally, I'd rather have the knowledge and never need it than need it and not have it.

So take what you have learned here and use it as an aid to learning about self-defense. Practice is the key. Drill both your mind and body until this sort of stuff becomes instinctive. Because that's the only way it'll ever become useful.

Afterword

I certainly hope that what you've learned here will keep you from getting your head caved in during a brawl. A lot of this stuff I learned by getting knocked upside the head by it. More of it I learned by having somebody pull it on me and having the gift of fast reflexes to escape. Much more of it I learned from my running buddies and other warriors.

I have walked a wild and woolly path in my life. It's unfortunate that the only "acceptable" way to be considered a warrior in our society is through the military, because most of our military has become a bureaucracy. If you're too wild to be a military pogue, there are not many ways to become a warrior that won't eventually lead you to the outlaw's path.

There have been good and bad times during my life on the outlaw path. Yet, sometimes I wonder what would have become of me if I hadn't decided to walk the roads I did. I don't cry about the cards life has dealt me, but sometimes I wonder how much of the shit I've gone through I could have avoided with a different outlook. One of my worst enemies for years was my temper. Yet, it was also one of my greatest (or so I thought at the time) strengths.

If you have a hot temper I'd like to bounce something off you (if you don't, read this anyway; it will tell you something about people who do). It may sound weird, but part of what really contributes to a bad temper is time. I used to have a nasty temper. I wasn't a yeller, I was a quiet mad. Normally, I'd be bopping around having a good time, fuckin' around and laughing with the folks. Every now and then, though, somebody would get bent about "that weird guy" and try and interject their own dose of how a man should behave. (What they didn't know was that I was laughing so hard because it hurt so much.) I was blowing off a lot of pain and anger by raising hell. These people discovered that weird translated into wolf real quick. Macho men suddenly discovered they had cornered a *real* "Animal"; not (like they had thought) some little guy who named himself, but somebody who really deserved the name. (By the way, I didn't name myself; I got it when I was a manager/bouncer of a restaurant near Venice.)

I used to say, "If I ever stopped laughing I'd kill somebody." While not entirely true, it wasn't exactly false either. It boiled down to the fact that unless I somehow managed to find a way to blow off the steam and heal myself, I was going to end up seriously dead. I never got to the point of direct suicide, but doing things like walking into a pool hall with a partner to take out an employee, with the calm understanding that the entire place would turn on us, wasn't the act of a totally sane person.

Fortunately, I found a key point to my temper. Time. We tend to look at it the wrong way in Western culture. People in the West tend to look at time as a one-point thing; they think of it as a line going from the past to the present to the future. The Orientals look at it in a circular fashion that extends in all directions. If you look around, most people either live in the past (glory days) or in the future (when I make it to the top). They try to escape the present, because the present is too painful (or so they think). Then there are people who are trapped in the present. This can get ugly.

Most people who live in the past make it out to be this wonderful time of happiness and joy. Part of what motivates them to do this is the fact that they didn't know then what they do now. In a real sense, they are wishing for ignorance. They want to go back to the time when they didn't know about the responsibility of living. Good luck. It doesn't work that way.

People who live in the future (those who are always planning and scheming what they're going to do next) are trying to run away from a painful past. It's like trying to run from your shadow; the faster you run, the faster it runs. These are the people who turn into alkies around forty because they've tried every scheme they could think of to escape the pain, but it's always stayed with them. What's the quote? Oh yeah, "Shit man, if I could drown my sorrows, I wouldn't have to drink."

The third sort are the people who have the worst tempers. These are people who are trapped in the here and now. They turned off the vision into the past because there is too much pain, and all they can see in the future is more of the same, so they've turned off that channel, too. These people have all sorts of pain that rides with them from the past, but it's become a blind spot. All they have are the feelings, but little memory or sight. This means whatever emotion they are having right now is all they can see. It rises up out of them and grabs them by the throat and balls and throws them across the room. These kind of people are totally caught by their emotions and have no constructive way to deal with them. The thing about these people is that they are time bombs waiting to go off. Some of them aren't looking for targets for this explosion, but some are. Those who aren't usually end up self-destructing somehow. Unless you're involved with them in some way, though, that's their problem. With those who are looking for a target, it can become your problem, because they want to make it your problem.

You must be able to spot these people, because anyone who is totally wrapped up in their emotions is not rational. When you're talking about fights, this is where it counts. The guy may blow a gasket and come after you. These people are dangerous. They're the types that pull weapons first or ambush you later with no other thought than to feed the emotional beast that has control of them at the moment. These are often the people who kill or get killed. Your job is not to get involved with them, unless you really want to be a corpse or a killer.

This state of mind is similar to what most people went through during their teens, when the world was suddenly much bigger than they thought it was and their hormones grabbed them by the nose and dragged them every which way. Unless some way is found to enlarge the person's world model so it can cope with this much input, they're going to eventually blow a gasket. Unfortunately, unlike adolescence, this stuff doesn't just settle down with the passing of a few years. It calls for some serious painful work to free yourself. This is something most people feel they can never do, so they stay there until one day they blow it somehow and the shit happens.

The thing is, the cops don't care why someone is like that. It doesn't matter to them that a person was abused as a child. What matters is that there is a body on the floor. If it's yours, well, you don't have to worry about it anymore. If it's the other guy's, your problems are just beginning.

This is why it is important to get a grip on your temper. You're entering an area where the ramifications of your actions can be serious. You look at it like your temper can't fuck up someone's life. It can. More than likely, it'll be yours. Sooner or later, the runway's going to run out on you, and payback is a bitch. So do yourself a favor and start working on your temper before it gets you killed.

By the way, the stuff in this book is not for fun either. This is not a lightweight game. Whether you're legal or illegal in your life doesn't matter; you're still playing for serious stakes with this stuff. I had a roommate who was a coroner in Miami. He used to body-bag people who thought it was for fun. Both of us have a knee-jerk reaction to the smell of blood these days because of that sort of thinking.

Anyway, now that I've told you why temper is a bad thing in regard to weapons, I think it would only be fair to give you some ideas of how to deal with it. Sort of like, "Well, I ripped your clothes off because they were full of bees, so I'd better give you a coat or something."

One of the hardest things for me to do was to escape the trap of the "here and now." Most of it had to do with healing myself. There are lots of ways to do it, and you have to find your own. (Unfortunately, the void can't be filled by alcohol or aerobics.) I had to look back and remember my past. There was a lot of ugly shit there that I didn't want to face. Thing is, as long as I didn't stop and spit in its eye, it kept chasing me into shit. I'd run from it and land in a brawl that would escalate into people hunting me. In order to survive, I'd have to fight, run, ambush, fight, run, ad nauseam. Before I got a grip on them, my mouth and temper kept getting me into shit. A lot of the time I would rather have had people shoot at me than look at what was going on inside.

Once I began to look back, I realized something real important. Those motherfuckers weren't right. They were assholes. The things they did to me and told me were bullshit. If they had lied to me about the past, then I could fuckin' well bet they had lied to me about the future. They had. So I began to look around and question all those definitions I had been given. You know, little things like right, wrong, good, bad, love, hate, men, women, and of course, me. After a couple of trips to Webster's, I discovered some pretty big mistakes in the definitions I had been given. The other thing I learned was that nobody I cared about died if I didn't use their definitions. If I changed for the better, Armageddon didn't happen. I just felt better about myself and life.

Once I began to question these definitions, I began to look towards the future. The future wasn't fixed as I had thought. Hell, if I changed where I was now, it would change where I was going to be in the future. The reason I thought it would cost too much to change is I had been told the price by people who wanted me to stay where they wanted me. This had nothing to do with where I had wanted to be. Until I started kickin' around though, I had no idea how big, varied, and exciting this world is. It ain't what you think it is out there. You aren't going to die if you change for the better. Nor are you going to be left alone forever.

It was then that I discovered something that made me howl with laughter. You want to know the absolute best way to get back at those bastards who fucked with your life? Heal yourself. By doing that you get to a point where they can't touch you. Even the very worst of them can sit there and spit poison, but it doesn't matter, because you've grown out of their range. You're a bigger person than they are. If you heal yourself, they can't touch you. Living a healthy, happy life will make them choke on their own poison better than anything else you could do.

What that all led to was the ability to blow off aggravations. My temper didn't rule me anymore. Hell, I wasn't trapped. If somebody was being an asshole, I could laugh it off. Man, until he was getting ready to move, it was *his* problem. If he started a move, I was there waiting for him. If something pissed me off, I could live through it—it wasn't forever. Sure, it was a pisser, but in ten minutes I'd be less pissed; in twenty, I'd have forgotten about it. This all sort of added up to me being able to mellow out. I started living my life the way I wanted to, not the way somebody else wanted me to live it. This meant fewer and fewer fights. Shit, these days I'm fat and sassy.

The main point is, you have to understand that *YOUR OWN TEMPER IS YOUR WORST ENEMY WHEN IT COMES TO WEAPONS!* I just explained to you how I know this. It's important for you to *really* know this, not only in your mind but down to your bones. *When it comes to weapon fighting you cannot afford to lose your cool.* If you do, you'll either bite off more than you can chew and get seriously hurt, or you'll dust somebody and get caught. You don't want either one to happen.

This is why you must keep a cool head whenever you think about using weapons. It's not a game, nor is it something that won't affect anything. Keep your eyes and mind open here, folks, because it is serious. You can get by pretty well if you're willing to accept that there's more to this movie called life than people commonly talk about. Most of the people who don't want to talk about it are using it against you anyway, so it's perfectly okay to be real suspicious about anybody telling you that something is or isn't a certain way. Learn to look into the shadows; they can be your friend. A lot of shadows hide under the name of the light, just as light hides in the darkness.

Don't change your address to the shadows of life, though. Real life consists of both light and darkness. If you let other people's shadows rule you, you'll never get out of this life alive.

So keep your minds and hearts open, folks, and try to live your life so you'll never need to apply the contents of this book. I mean, hell, sex is more fun than fighting anyway—go get laid instead!

About the Author

Marc "Animal" MacYoung is one of those individuals who can be best summed up as bizarre. It is not an insult; it's because the word eclectic doesn't cover enough territory to describe him. He's a walking blend of philosopher, biker, intellectual, shitkicker, handyman, martial artist, thug, mystic, wolf, and total loonytoon. His personality consists of varying depths and levels, and his interests fall within a wide range. A self-professed "asshole when younger," he came about his knowledge from actual hard experience, as well as formal training.

The actual number of fights and women Animal has won is lost in the mists of time. This is because he quit "keeping score" about ten years ago. If pressed, however, he admits to winning more women than fights, and there are more than thirty fights (for sure, it gets into hazy definitions after that).

He's currently living in the L.A. area with his lady, Tracy, two cats, and a varying number of roommates. This is interrupted by forays out into the rest of the country when the mood strikes him (or he's not broke).